Alfred Monnin, John Edward Bowden

The Spirit of the Curé of Ars

Alfred Monnin, John Edward Bowden

The Spirit of the Curé of Ars

ISBN/EAN: 9783743484030

Manufactured in Europe, USA, Canada, Australia, Japa

Cover: Foto ©Lupo / pixelio.de

Manufactured and distributed by brebook publishing software (www.brebook.com)

Alfred Monnin, John Edward Bowden

The Spirit of the Curé of Ars

THE SPIRIT

OF

THE CURÉ OF ARS.

Translated from the French of

M. L'ABBÉ MONNIN.

WITH SEVENTEEN ADDITIONAL EXHORTATIONS.

EDITED BY

JOHN EDWARD BOWDEN,

PRIEST OF THE ORATORY OF ST. PHILIP NERI.

Authorised Translation.

LONDON:
BURNS, LAMBERT, AND OATES,
17 AND 18 PORTMAN STREET,
AND 63 PATERNOSTER ROW.

1865.

LONDON:
LEVEY AND CO., PRINTERS, GREAT NEW STREET,
FETTER LANE, E.C.

PREFACE.

THE following pages have been translated, by the kind permission of the Abbé Monnin, from the small volume lately published by him, under the title of *Esprit du Curé d'Ars*. To this it has been thought well to add the exhortations of M. Vianney, given in a book called, *Ars : ou, Le Jeune Philosophe redevenu Chrétien*, and published by Perisse Frères, in 1856.

The devotion to the holy Curé of Ars is now so widely spread in England, that a few words concerning the present state of the scene of his labours may be found acceptable.

All is as he left it but five years ago. The little church remains unchanged, except that his body lies beneath a black slab in the centre of its nave; for the magnificent chapel of St. Philomena, which was planned under his direction, will not be completed before next year. Altar and chair, pulpit and confessional, remain as he used them, to recall the inspired words and the heroic life which made the once neglected church of Ars one of the favourite pilgrimages of Europe. That pilgrimage is continued now; and scarcely a week passes without some miraculous events, to reward the faith of those who perform it, and to show that his blessing rests upon it still.

Ars is visited by considerable numbers of persons at all times of the year; but especially about the 4th of August, the anniversary of the death of M. Vianney. The daily morning and evening instructions are carried on by the missionaries whom he associated with himself in his work; and the Retreats which he founded are still given twice in every month.

The few objects which the holy Curé used are collected together in his room, to the door of which the faithful are admitted. The uneven staircase and brick floor, the rough lantern and earthenware pipkin, are characteristic of him in whose mouth "poor" was the favourite epithet for all belonging to himself; while the embroidered vestments, jewelled chalices, and marble altars, bespeak his love for the beauty of the house of God.

Those who knew him intimately for many years are there to speak of his holiness. The missionaries who shared his labours, the Brother of the

Holy Family who was constantly at his side, and the devout persons whose privilege it was to serve him, bear joyful witness to wonders which fell under their own observation, and to that supernatural life of their Pastor which was the greatest miracle of all.

It is understood that the Holy Father has expressed great interest in the Beatification of the Curé of Ars, and has desired that his cause may be introduced to the Roman Congregation as soon as possible. The devotion of the people, who regard him as a saint, has rendered it necessary to remove the railings which at first surrounded his tomb; and the *ex-voto* offerings with which they were abundantly covered have been reserved until the time when the Church shall authorise such public expressions of veneration.

If we have ever thought, in reading of the apostolic labours of saints who lived in times gone by, that the uncompromising severity of their teaching would have been modified by the altered circumstances of our own age, the life of the Curé of Ars shows us that we were mistaken. We see him in the midst of a neighbouring people, the trusted guide of every class of Christians. Every doubt that could arise from the exigencies of the nineteenth century, concerning theology, politics, or even fashion, was submitted to his decision; and he answered one and all in words which might have fallen from St. Vincent Ferrer or the B. Leonard of Port Maurice. Thus, when we hear of the numbers of all ranks and conditions who crowded from town and country into the secluded village church to hear his simple exhortations, our thoughts go back to the time when Pharisees and Sadducees, soldiers and publicans, thronged the desert-banks of the Jordan to hear the preaching of St. John Baptist, and to be told that they must do penance, because the kingdom of heaven was at hand.

In perusing the instructions of the Curé of Ars, we may miss the sweetness of his voice, or the bright look and affectionate manner with which they were wont to be accompanied; but our hearts burn within us as we read, for they come from a saint on fire with the love of God, who was raised up in an unbelieving generation to carry on the old tradition, and to sanctify the world by the simple preaching of the Cross.

JOHN E. BOWDEN.

THE ORATORY, LONDON,
    Feast of St. Elisabeth, 1864.

CONTENTS.

PART I.

THE CURÉ OF ARS IN HIS CATECHISMS, p. 1.

SECT.		PAGE
I.	Catechism on Salvation	36
II.	Catechism on the Love of God	39
III.	Catechism on the Prerogatives of the Pure Soul	43
IV.	Catechism on the Holy Spirit	47
V.	Catechism on the Blessed Virgin	53
VI.	Catechism on the Sanctification of Sunday	57
VII.	Catechism on the Word of God	59
VIII.	Catechism on Prayer	65
IX.	Catechism on the Priesthood	69
X.	Catechism on the Holy Sacrifice of the Mass	74
XI.	Catechism on the Real Presence	77
XII.	Catechism on Communion	80
XIII.	Catechism on Frequent Communion	83
XIV.	Catechism on Sin	88
XV.	On the same Subject	92
XVI.	Catechism on Pride	96
XVII.	Catechism on Impurity	99
XVIII.	Catechism on Confession	102
XIX.	Catechism on the Cardinal Virtues	106
XX.	Catechism on Hope	111
XXI.	Catechism on Suffering	113

PART II.

THE CURÉ OF ARS IN HIS HOMILIES, p. 123.

I.	Homily on the Parable of the Cockle	129
II.	Homily on the Parable of the Labourers	131
III.	Homily on the Gospel for the First Sunday in Lent	133
IV.	Homily on the Gospel for the Twenty-first Sunday after Pentecost	140
V.	Homily for the last Sunday in the Year	146

PART III.

SECT.		PAGE
I.	The Curé of Ars in his Conversation	151
II.	Faith of M. Vianney	173
III.	Hope of M. Vianney	176
IV.	Charity of M. Vianney	180
V.	Thoughts of M. Vianney on the Joys of the Interior Life	186
VI.	Zeal of M. Vianney	193
VII.	Love of M. Vianney for the Poor	198
VIII.	Humility of M. Vianney	201
IX.	Thoughts of M. Vianney on Self-denial and Suffering	207
X.	How M. Vianney spoke of the Saints	210

PART IV.

SEVENTEEN EXHORTATIONS OF THE CURÉ OF ARS.

I.		215
II.	On Death	219
III.	On the Last Judgment	222
IV.	On Sin	226
V.	On Temptations	230
VI.	On Pride	232
VII.	On Avarice	236
VIII.	On Luxury	239
IX.	On Envy	241
X.	On Gluttony	243
XI.	On Anger	247
XII.	On Sloth	249
XIII.	On Grace	252
XIV.	On Habitual Grace	256
XV.	On Prayer	259
XVI.	On the Love of God	263
XVII.	On Paradise	270

SPIRIT OF THE CURÉ OF ARS.

PART I.

THE CURÉ OF ARS IN HIS CATECHISMS.

"THERE is no doubt," says Père Gratry, "that, through purity of heart, innocence, either preserved or recovered by virtue, faith, and religion, there are in man capabilities and resources of mind, of body, and of heart which most people would not suspect. To this order of resources belongs what theology calls infused science, the intellectual virtues which the Divine Word inspires into our minds when He dwells in us by faith and love."

And the learned Oratorian quotes with enthusiasm, excusing himself for not translating them better, these magnificent words of a saint who lived in the eleventh century, in one of the mystic monasteries on the banks of the Rhine:

"This is what purifies the eye of the heart, and enables it to raise itself to the true light: contempt of worldly cares, mortification of the body, contrition of heart, abundance of tears, ... meditation on the admirable Essence of God and on His chaste Truth, fervent and pure prayer, joy in God, ardent desire of heaven. Embrace all this," adds the saint, "and continue in it. Advance towards the light which offers itself to you as to its sons, and descends of itself into your hearts. Take your hearts out of your breasts, and give them to Him who speaks to you, and He will fill them with deific splendour, and you will be sons of light and angels of God."

The description we have just read seems to have been traced from the very life of the Curé of Ars. Every detail recalls him, every feature harmonises marvellously with his. Who has ever carried further " contempt of worldly cares, mortification of the body, abundance of tears"? He was always bathed in tears. And then, " meditation on the admirable Essence of God and on His chaste Truth, and fervent and pure prayer, joy in God, ardent desire of heaven,"— how characteristic is this! " He had advanced towards the light, and the light had descended of itself into his heart. . . . He had taken his heart from his breast, and given it to Him who spoke to him; and He who spoke to him," who is the Divine, uncreated Word of God, "filled him with deific splendour." No one could doubt it who has had the happiness of assisting at any of the catechisms of Ars; of hearing that extraordinary language, which was like no human language; who has seen the irresistible effect produced upon hearers of all classes by that voice, that emotion, that intuition, that fire, and the signal beauty of that unpolished and almost vulgar French, which was transfigured and penetrated by his holy energy, even to the form, the arrangement, and the harmony of its words and syllables. And yet the Curé of Ars did not speak *words;* true eloquence consists in speaking things: he spoke things, and in a most wonderful manner. He poured out his whole soul into the souls of the crowds who listened to him, that he might make them believe, love, and hope like himself. That is the aim and the triumph of evangelical eloquence.

How could this man, who had nearly been refused admittance into the great Seminary because of his ignorance, and who had, since his promotion to the priesthood, been solely employed in prayer and in the labours of the confessional—how could he have attained to the power of teaching doctrine like one of the Fathers of the Church? Whence did he derive his astonishing knowledge of God, of nature, and of the history of the soul? How was it that his thoughts and expressions so often coincided with those of the greatest Christian geniuses, St. Augustine, St. Bernard, St. Thomas Aquinas, St. Catherine of Siena, St. Teresa?

For example, we have often heard him say that the heart of the saints was *liquid*. We were much struck with this energetic expression, without suspecting that it was so theologically accurate; and we were surprised and touched to find, in turning over the pages of the *Summa*, that the angelical doctor assigns to love four immediate effects, of which the first is the *liquefaction* of the heart. M. Vianney had certainly never read St. Thomas, which makes this coincidence the more remarkable; and, indeed, it is inexplicable to those who are ignorant of the workings of grace, and who do not comprehend those words of the Divine Master: " Thou hast hid these things from the wise and prudent, and hast revealed them to little ones."*

The Spirit of God had been pleased to engrave on the heart of this holy priest all that he was to know and to teach to others; and it was the more deeply engraved, as that heart was the more pure, the more detached, and

* St. Matt. xi. 25.

empty of the vain science of men; like a clean and polished block of marble, ready for the tool of the sculptor.

The faith of the Curé of Ars was his whole science; his book was our Lord Jesus Christ. He sought for wisdom nowhere but in Jesus Christ, in His death and in His cross. To him no other wisdom was true, no other wisdom useful. He sought it not amid the dust of libraries, not in the schools of the learned, but in prayer, on his knees, at his Master's Feet, covering His Divine Feet with tears and kisses; in the presence of the holy tabernacles, where he passed his days and nights before the crowd of pilgrims had yet deprived him of liberty day and night, he had learnt it all.

When persons have heard him discourse upon heaven, on the Sacred Humanity of our Lord, on his dolorous Passion, His Real Presence in the most Holy Sacrament of our altars, on the Blessed Virgin Mary, her attractions and her greatness, on the happiness of the saints, the purity of the angels, the beauty of souls, the dignity of man,—on all those subjects which were familiar to him,—it often happened to them to come out from the discourse quite convinced that the good father *saw* the things of which he had spoken with such fulness of heart, with such eloquent emotion, in such passionate accents, with such abundance of tears; and indeed his words were then impressed with a character of divine tenderness, of sweet gentleness, and of penetrating unction, which was beyond all comparison. There was so extraordinary a majesty, so marvellous a power, in his voice, in his gestures, in his looks, in his transfigured countenance, that it was impossible to listen to him and remain cold and unmoved.

Views and thoughts imparted by a divine light have quite a different bearing from those acquired by study. Doubt was dispelled from the most rebellious hearts, and the admirable clearness of faith took its place, before so absolute a certainty, an exposition at once so luminous and so simple.

The word of the Curé of Ars was the more efficacious, because he preached with his whole being. His mere presence was a manifestation of the truth; and of him it might well be said, that he would have moved and convinced men even by his silence. When there appeared in the pulpit that pale, thin, and transparent face; when you heard that shrill, piercing voice, like a cry, giving out to the crowd sublime thoughts clothed in simple and popular language,—you fancied yourself in the presence of one of those great characters of the Bible, speaking to men in the language of the prophets. You were already filled with respect and confidence, and disposed to listen, not for enjoyment, but for profit.

Before he began, the venerable catechist used to cast a glance over his hearers, which prepared the way for his word. Sometimes this glance became fixed on some one; it seemed to be searching into the depths of some soul which the saint had suddenly seen through, and in which one would have thought he was looking for the text of his discourse. How many have thought he was speaking to them alone! How many have recognised themselves in the picture he drew of their weaknesses! How many have listened to the secret history of their failings, of their temptations, of their combats, of their uneasiness, and of their remorse!

To those to whom it was given to assist at these catechisms, two things were equally remarkable—the preacher and the hearer. It was not words that the preacher gave forth,—it was more than words; it was a soul, a holy soul, all filled with faith and love, that poured itself out before you, of which you felt in your own soul the immediate contact and the warmth. As for the hearer, he was no longer on the earth, he was transported into those pure regions from which dogmas and mysteries descend. As the saint spoke, new and clear views opened to the mind; heaven and earth, the present and the future life, the things of time and of eternity, appeared in a light that you had never before perceived.

When a man, coming fresh from the world, and bringing with him worldly ideas, feelings, and impressions, sat down to listen to this doctrine, it stunned and amazed him—it set so utterly at defiance the world, and all that the world believes, loves, and extols. At first he was astonished and thunderstruck; then by degrees he was touched, and surprised into weeping like the rest. No eloquence has drawn forth more tears, or penetrated deeper into the hearts of men. His words opened a way before them like flames, and the most hardened hearts melted like wax before the fire. They were burning, radiating, triumphant; they did more than charm the mind, —they subdued the whole soul, and brought it back to God, not by the long and difficult way of argument, but by the paths of emotion, which lead shortly and directly to the desired end.

M. Vianney was listened to as a new apostle, sent by Jesus Christ to His Church, to renew in her the holiness and fervour of His Divine

Spirit, in an age whose corruption has so effaced them from the souls of most men. And it is a great marvel that, proposing, like the Apostles, a doctrine incomprehensible to human reason, and very bitter to the depraved taste of the world,—speaking of nothing but crosses, humiliations, poverty, and penance,—his doctrine was so well received. Those who had not yet received it into their hearts were glad to feed their mind upon it. If they had not courage to make it the rule of their conduct, they could not help admiring and wishing to follow it.

It is not less remarkable that, though he spoke only in the incorrect and common French natural to people brought up in the country, one might say of him, as of the Apostles, that he was heard by all the nations of the world, and that his voice resounded through all the earth. He was the oracle that people went to consult, that they might learn to know Jesus Christ. Not only the simple but the learned, not only the fervent but the indifferent, found in it a divine unction which penetrated them, and made them long to hear it again. The more they heard, the more they wished to hear; and they always came back with love to the foot of that pulpit, as to a place where they had found beauty and truth. Nothing more clearly showed that the Curé of Ars was full of the Spirit of God, Who alone is greater than our heart; we may draw from His depths without ever exhausting them, and the divine satiety which He gives only excites a greater appetite.

The holy Curé spoke without any other preparation than his continual union with God; he passed without any interval or delay from the confessional to the pulpit; and yet he showed an imperturbable confidence, which sprang from complete and absolute forgetfulness of himself. Besides, no one was tempted to criticise him. People generally criticise those who are not indifferent to their opinion of them. Those who heard the Curé of Ars had something else to do—they had to pass judgment on themselves.

M. Vianney cared nothing for what might be said or thought of him. Of whomsoever his audience might consist, though Bishops and other illustrious personages often mingled with the crowd that surrounded his pulpit, he never betrayed the least emotion, nor the least embarrassment proceeding from human respect. He, who was so timid and so humble, was no longer the same person when he passed through the compact mass that filled the church at the hour of catechism; he wore an air of triumph, he carried his head high, his face was lighted up, and his eyes cast brilliant glances.

He was asked one day if he had never been afraid of his audience. "No," he answered; "on the contrary, the more people there are, the better I am pleased." Then, to impose on us, he added, "A proud man always thinks he does well." If he had had the Pope, the Cardinals, and Kings around his pulpit, he would have said neither more nor less, for he thought only of souls, and made them think only of God. This real power of his word supplied in him the want of talent and rhetoric; it gave a singular majesty and an irresistible authority to the most simple things that issued from that venerable mouth.

The power of his word was also increased by the high opinion the pilgrims entertained of his sanctity. "The first quality of the man called to the perilous honour of instructing the people," says St. Isidore, "is to be holy and irreproachable.' He whose mission it is to deter others from sin must be a stranger to sin; he whose task it is to lead others to perfection must be in every thing their model of perfection." In the holy catechist of Ars, virtue was preaching truth. When he spoke of the love of God, of humility, gentleness, patience, mortification, sacrifice, poverty, or the desire of suffering, his example gave immense weight to his words; for a man who practises what he teaches is very powerful in convincing and persuading others.

He used to put his ideas into the most simple and transparent form, letting them suggest the expression that best suited them. He could bring truths of the highest order within the reach of every intellect; he clothed them in familiar language; his simplicity touched the heart, and his doctrine delighted the mind. That science which is not sought for is abundant; it flows like the fountain of living water, which the Samaritan woman knew not, and of which the Saviour taught her the virtue. Thus, his considerations on sin, on the offence it is against God, and the evil it inflicts on man, were the painful result of his thoughts. They penetrated him, they overwhelmed him; they were like a burning arrow piercing his breast; he relieved his pain by giving utterance to it.

It was a wonderful thing that this man, so ready to proclaim his own ignorance, had by nature a great attraction for the higher faculties of the mind. The greatest praise that he could give any one was to say that he was clever. When the good qualities of any great person, whether an ecclesiastic or a layman, were enumerated before him, he seldom failed to complete the panegyric in these words: "What pleases me most is, that he is learned."

M. Vianney appreciated the gift of eloquence in others; he blessed God, who, for His own glory, gives such privileges to man, but he disdained them for himself. He had no scruple in utterly neglecting grammar and syntax in his discourses; he seemed to do it on purpose, out of humility, for there were faults in them that he might easily have avoided. But this incorrect language penetrated the souls of his hearers—enlightened and converted them. "A polished discourse," says St. Jerome, "only gratifies the ears; one which is not so makes its way to the heart."

His manner of speaking was sudden and impetuous; he loosed his words like arrows from a bow, and his whole soul seemed to fly with them. In these effusions the pathetic, the profound, the sublime, was often side by side with the simple and the vulgar. They had all the freedom and irregularity, but also all the originality and power, of an improvisation. We have sometimes tried to write down what we had just heard, but it was impossible to recall the things that had most moved us, and to put them into form. What is most divine in the heart of man cannot be expressed in writing.

We have, however, set down a few words, in which we find more than an echo or a remembrance. We find the Curé of Ars himself, the simple expression of his heart and of his soul. These are some of his lofty and deep thoughts:

"To love God! oh, how beautiful it is! We must be in heaven to comprehend love. . . . Prayer helps us a little, because prayer is the elevation of the soul to heaven. . . .

"The more we know men, the less we love them. It is the reverse with God; the more we know Him, the more we love Him. This knowledge inflames the soul with such a love, that it can no longer love or desire any thing but God. . . . Man was created by love; therefore he is so disposed to love. On the other hand, he is so great that nothing on the earth can satisfy him. He can be satisfied only when he turns towards God. . . . Take a fish out of the water, and it will not live. Well, such is man without God.

"There are some who do not love the good God, who do not pray to Him, and who prosper; that is a bad sign. They have done a little good in the midst of a great deal of evil. The good God rewards them in this life.

"This earth is a bridge to cross the water; it serves only to support our steps. . . . We are in this world, but we are not of this world, since we say every day, 'Our Father, who art in heaven.' . . . We must wait, then, for our reward till we are *at home*, in our Father's house. This is the reason why good Christians suffer crosses, contradictions, adversities, contempt, calumnies—so much the better! . . . But people are astonished at this. They seem to think that because we love the good God a little, we ought to have nothing to contradict us, nothing to make us suffer. . . . We say, 'There is a person who is not good, and yet every thing goes well with him; but with me, it is of no use doing my best; every thing goes wrong.' It is because we do not understand the value and the happiness of crosses. We say sometimes, God chastises those whom He loves. That is not true. Trials are not chastisements; they are graces to those whom God loves. . . . We must not consider the labour, but the recompense. A merchant does not consider the trouble he undergoes in his commerce, but the profit he gains by it. . . . What are twenty years, thirty years, compared to eternity? What, then, have we to suffer? A few humiliations, a few annoyances, a few sharp words; *that will not kill us.*

"It is glorious to be able to please God, so little as we are!

"Our tongue should be employed only in

praying, our heart in loving, our eyes in weeping.

"We are great, and we are nothing.... There is nothing greater than man, and nothing less. Nothing is greater, if we consider his soul; nothing is less, if we look at his body.... We occupy ourselves with the body, as if we had it alone to take care of; we have, on the contrary, it alone to despise....

"We are the work of a God: ... one always loves one's own work.... It is easy enough to understand that we are the work of a God; but that the crucifixion of a God should be our work! that is incomprehensible....

"Some people attribute a hard heart to the Eternal Father. Oh, how mistaken they are! The Eternal Father, to disarm His own justice, gave to His Son an excessively tender heart; no one can give what he does not possess.

"Our Lord said to His Father: 'Father, do not punish them!' ...

"Our Lord suffered more than was necessary to redeem us. But what would have satisfied the justice of His Father would not have satisfied His love. Without our Lord's Death, all mankind together could not expiate a single little lie.

"In the world, people hide heaven and hell: heaven, because if we knew its beauty, we should wish to go there at all costs—we should, indeed, leave the world alone; hell, because if we knew the torments that are endured there, we should do all we could to avoid going there.

"The sign of the cross is formidable to the devil, because by the Cross we escape from him. . . . We should make the sign of the cross with great respect. We begin with the forehead: it is the head, creation—the Father; then the heart: love, life, redemption—the Son; then the shoulders: strength—the Holy Ghost. . . .

"Every thing reminds us of the Cross. We ourselves are made in the form of a cross.

"In heaven we shall be nourished by the breath of God. . . . The good God will place us as an architect places the stones of a building—each one in the spot to which it is adapted.

"The souls of the saints contained the foundations of heaven. They felt an emanation from heaven, in which they bathed and lost themselves. . . . As the disciples on Mount Thabor saw nothing but Jesus alone, so interior souls, on the Thabor of their hearts, no longer see any thing but our Lord. They are two friends, who are never tired of each other. . . .

"There are some who lose the faith, and never see hell till they enter it.

"The lost will be enveloped in the wrath of God, as the fish are in the water.

"It is not God who condemns us to hell; it is we ourselves who do it by our sins. The lost do not accuse God; they accuse themselves. They say, 'I have lost God, my soul, and heaven by my own fault.'

"No one was ever lost for having done too much evil; but many are in hell for a single mortal sin of which they would not repent.

"If a lost soul could say once, 'O my God, I love Thee!' there would be no more hell for him; . . . but, alas, poor soul! it has lost the power of loving which it had received, and of which it made no use. Its heart is dried up like grapes that have passed through the wine-press. No more joy in that soul, no more peace, because there is no more love. . . .

"Hell has its origin in the goodness of God. The lost will say, 'Oh, if at least God had not loved us so much, we should suffer less! Hell would be endurable. . . . But to have been so much loved! what grief!'"

Beside these deep thoughts, he had some that were forcible and startling. He called the cemetery, the home of all; purgatory, the infirmary of the good God; the earth, a warehouse.

"We are on the earth," he said, "only as in

a warehouse, for a very little moment. . . . We seem not to move, and we are going towards eternity as if by steam.

"A dying man was asked what should be put on his tomb. He answered, 'You shall put, Here lies a fool, who went out of this world without knowing how he came into it.'

"If the poor lost souls had the time that we waste, what good use they would make of it! If they had only half an hour, that half-hour would depopulate hell.

"In dying, we make restitution; we restore to the earth what it gave us—a little pinch of dust, the size of a nut; that is what we shall become. There is, indeed, much to be proud of in that!

"For our body, death is only a cleansing. In this world we must labour, we must fight. We shall have plenty of time to rest in all eternity.

"If we understood our happiness aright, we might almost say that we are happier than the saints in heaven. They live upon their income: they can earn no more; while we can augment our treasure every moment.

"The Commandments of God are the guides which God gives us to show us the road to heaven; like the names written up at the corners of the streets and on guide-posts, to point out the way.

"The grace of God helps us to walk, and supports us. He is as necessary to us as crutches are to a lame man.

"When we go to confession, we ought to understand what we are going to do. It might be said that we are going to unfasten our Lord from the cross. When you have made a good confession, you have chained up the devil. The sins that we conceal will all come to light. In order to conceal our sins effectually, we must confess them thoroughly. Our faults are like a grain of sand beside the great mountain of the mercies of the good God."

M. Vianney made great use of comparisons and similes in his teaching; he borrowed them from nature, which was known and loved by the crowd whom he addressed, from the beauties of the country, from the emotions of rural life. The recollections of his childhood had kept all their freshness, and in his old age he could not resist the innocent pleasure of recalling for a moment the lively sympathies of his youth. This return of the thoughts to the brightest days of life is like an anticipation of the resurrection. After the manner of our Lord, he used the most well-known events, the most common facts, the incidents that came before him, as figures of the spiritual life, and made them the theme of his instructions. The

Gospel is full of symbols and figures, fitted to lead the soul to the comprehension of eternal truths by a comparison with what is more evident to the senses. In like manner, allusions, metaphors, parables, and figures, coloured all the discourses of the Curé of Ars. His mind had acquired the habit of raising itself, by means of visible things, to God and to the invisible. There was not one of his catechisms in which he did not often speak of rivulets, forests, trees, birds, flowers, dew, lilies, balm, perfume, and honey. All contemplatives love this language, and the innocence of their thoughts attaches itself by predilection to all the beautiful and pure things with which the Author of creation has embellished His work. A good man, our Lord says, brings forth good things out of the good treasure of his heart. The sweet writings of St. Francis of Sales are a model of this style, dear to all mystics; and we are not surprised to find these graces of language and this exquisite taste in the Bishop of Geneva. But where had this poor country curé learnt his flowers of eloquence? Who had taught him to use them with such delicate tact and ingenuity? Let us listen:

"Like a beautiful white dove rising from the midst of the waters, and coming to shake her wings over the earth, the Holy Spirit issues from the infinite ocean of the Divine perfections, and hovers over pure souls, to pour into them the balm of love.

"The Holy Spirit reposes in a pure soul as on a bed of roses. There comes forth from a soul in which the Holy Spirit resides a sweet odour, like that of the vine when it is in flower.

"He who has preserved his baptismal innocence is like a child who has never disobeyed his father. . . .

"One who has kept his innocence feels himself lifted up on high by love, as a bird is carried up by its wings. Those who have pure souls are like eagles and swallows, which fly in the air. . . . A Christian who is pure is upon earth like a bird that is kept fastened down by a string. Poor little bird! it only waits for the moment when the string is cut to fly away.

"Good Christians are like those birds that have large wings and small feet, and which never light upon the ground, because they could not rise again, and would be caught. They make their nests, too, upon the points of rocks, on the roofs of houses, in high places. So the Christian ought to be always on the heights. As soon as we lower our thoughts towards the earth, we are taken captive.

"A pure soul is like a fine pearl. As long as it is hidden in the shell, at the bottom of the sea, no one thinks of admiring it. But if you bring it into the sunshine, this pearl will shine and attract all eyes. Thus, the pure soul, which is hidden from the eyes of the world, will one day shine before the angels in the sunshine of eternity.

"The pure soul is a beautiful rose, and the Three Divine Persons descend from heaven to inhale its fragrance.

"The mercy of God is like an overflowing torrent—it carries away hearts with it as it passes.

"The good God will pardon a repentant sinner more quickly than a mother would snatch her child out of the fire.

"The elect are like the ears of corn that are left by the reapers, and like the bunches of grapes after the vintage.

"Imagine a poor mother obliged to let fall the blade of the guillotine upon the head of her child: such is the good God when He condemns a sinner.

"What happiness will it be for the just, at the end of the world, when the soul, perfumed with the odours of heaven, shall be reunited to its body, and enjoy God for all eternity! Then our bodies will come out of the ground like linen that has been bleached. . . . The bodies of the just will shine in heaven like fine diamonds, like globes of love!

"What a cry of joy when the soul shall come to unite itself to its glorified body—to that body which will never more be to it an instrument of sin, nor a cause of suffering! It will revel in the sweetness of love, as the bee revels in flowers. . . . Thus the soul will be embalmed for eternity!" . . .

We see that the Curé of Ars was a poet, in the highest sense of the word; for his heart was endowed with exquisite sensibility, and he gave expression to it in the simplest and truest manner.

"One day in spring," he said, "I was going to see a sick person; the bushes were full of little birds, that were singing with all their might. I took pleasure in listening to them, and I said to myself, 'Poor little birds, you know not what you are doing! What a pity that is! You are singing the praises of God.'"

Does not this recall St. Francis of Assisi?

"Our holy Curé," writes one of his most intelligent hearers, "is always equally admirable in his life, his works, and his words. This may perhaps surprise you, but it is perfectly true. There is something astonishing in the satisfaction, or rather the enthusiasm, with which the crowd of all classes presses in to hear his so-called catechisms. I have heard distinguished ecclesiastics, men of the world, learned men, and artists, declare that nothing had ever touched them so much as that expansion of a heart which contemplates, which loves, which sighs, and which adores. A collection might almost be made of the *Fioretti* of the Curé of Ars. Nothing could be more graceful and brilliant than the picture he drew, a few days ago, of spring."

A few lines further on, he added, "Yesterday, our old St. Francis of Assisi was more poetical than ever, in the midst of his tears and of his bursts of love. Speaking of the soul of man, which ought to aspire to God alone, he cried out, 'Does the fish seek the trees and the fields? No; it darts through the water. Does the bird remain on the earth? No; it flies in the air. . . . And man, who is created to love God, to possess God, to contain God, what will he do with all the powers that have been given him for that end?'"

He liked to relate the simple and poetic legend of St. Maur, who, when he was one day carrying St. Benedict his dinner, found a large serpent. He took it up, put it in the fold of his habit, and showed it to St. Benedict, saying,

"See, father, what I have found." When the holy patriarch and all the religious were assembled, the serpent began to hiss, and try to bite them. Then St. Benedict said, "My child, go back, and put it where you found it." And when St. Maur was gone, he added, "My brethren, do you know why that animal is so gentle with that child? It is because he has kept his baptismal innocence."

He also repeated with great pleasure the anecdote of St. Francis of Assisi preaching to the fishes. "One day," he said, "St. Francis of Assisi was preaching in a province where there were a great many heretics. These miscreants stopped their ears to avoid hearing him. The saint then led the people to the sea-shore, and called the fishes to come and listen to the Word of God, since men rejected it. The fishes came to the edge of the water, the large ones behind the little ones. St. Francis asked them this question, 'Are you grateful to the good God for saving you from the deluge?' The fishes bowed their heads. Then St. Francis said to the people, 'See, these fishes are grateful for the benefits of God, and you are so ungrateful as to despise them!'"

M. Vianney mingled with his discourses some happy reminiscences of his shepherd's life:

"We ought to do like shepherds who are in

the fields in winter,—life is indeed a long winter. They kindle a fire, but from time to time they run about in all directions to look for wood to keep it up. If we, like the shepherds, were always to keep up the fire of the love of God in our hearts by prayers and good works, it would never go out.

"If you have not the love of God, you are very poor. You are like a tree without flowers or fruit.

"It is always spring-time in a soul united to God."

When he spoke of prayer, the most pleasing and ingenious comparisons fell abundantly from his lips:

"Prayer is a fragrant dew; but we must pray with a pure heart to feel this dew.

"There flows from prayer a delicious sweetness, like the juice of very ripe grapes.

"Prayer disengages our soul from matter; it raises it on high, like the fire that inflates a balloon.

"The more we pray, the more we wish to pray. Like a fish which at first swims on the surface of the water, and afterwards plunges down, and is always going deeper, the soul plunges, dives, and loses itself in the sweetness of conversing with God.

"Time never seems long in prayer. I know

not whether we can even wish for heaven? Oh, yes! . . . The fish swimming in a little rivulet is well off, because it is in its element; but it is still better in the sea. When we pray, we should open our heart to God, like a fish when it sees the wave coming.

"The good God has no need of us. He commands us to pray only because He wills our happiness, and our happiness can be found only in prayer. When He sees us coming, He bends His heart down very low towards His little creature, as a father bends down to listen to his little child when it speaks to him.

"In the morning, we must do like the little child in its cradle. The moment it opens its eyes, it looks round the house for its mother. When it sees her, it begins to smile; if it does not see her, it cries."

Speaking of the priest, he made use of this touching simile:

"The priest is like a mother to you, like a nurse to a child of a few months old. She feeds it—it has only to open its mouth. The mother says to her child, 'Here, my little one, eat.' The priest says to you, 'Take and eat; this is the Body of Jesus Christ. May it keep you, and lead you to life eternal.' Oh, beautiful words! . . .'

"A child, when it sees its mother, springs towards her; it struggles against any one who keeps it back; it opens its little mouth, and stretches out its little arms to embrace her. Your soul, in the presence of the priest, naturally springs towards him; it runs to meet him; but it is held back by the bonds of the flesh, in men who give every thing to the senses, who live only for their carcass.

"Our soul is swathed in our body, like a baby in its swaddling-clothes; we can see nothing but its face."

Every one will be struck with the truth and aptitude of this last simile. Beside these touching comparisons, some of M. Vianney's were original and energetic. To exalt the benefits of the Sacrament of Penance, he made use of metaphors and parables:

"A furious wolf once came into our country, devouring every thing. Finding on its way a child of two years old, he seized it in his mouth, and carried it off; but some men, who were pruning a vineyard, ran to attack him, and snatched his prey from him. It is thus that the Sacrament of Penance snatches us from the claws of the devil."

When he had to draw a parallel between Christians and worldly people, he said:

"I think none so much to be pitied as

those poor worldly people. They wear a cloak lined with thorns—they cannot move without pricking themselves; while good Christians have a cloak lined with soft fur.

"The good Christian sets no value on the goods of this world. He escapes from them like a rat out of the water.

"Unhappily, our hearts are not sufficiently pure and free from all earthly affections. If you take a very clean and very dry sponge, and soak it in water, it will be filled to overflowing; but if it is not dry and clean, it will take up nothing. In like manner, when the heart is not free and disengaged from the things of earth, it is in vain that we steep it in prayer; it will absorb nothing.

"The heart of the wicked swarms with sins like an ant-hill with ants. It is like a piece of bad meat full of worms.

"When we abandon ourselves to our passions, we interweave thorns around our heart.

"We are like moles of a week old; no sooner do we see the light, than we bury ourselves in the ground.

"The devil amuses us till the last moment, as a poor man is kept amused while the soldiers are coming to take him. When they come, he cries and struggles in vain, for they will not release him.

"When men die, they are often like a very rusty bar of iron, that must be put into the fire.

"Poor sinners are stupefied like snakes in winter.

"The slanderer is like the snail, which, crawling over flowers, leaves its slime upon them and defiles them.

"What would you say of a man who should plough his neighbour's field, and leave his own uncultivated? Well, that is what you do. You are always at work on the consciences of others, and you leave your own untilled. Oh, when death comes, how we shall regret having thought so much of others, and so little of ourselves; for we shall have to give an account of ourselves, and not of others! . . . Let us think of ourselves, of our own conscience, which we ought always to examine, as we examine our hands to see if they are clean.

"We always have two secretaries: the devil, who writes down our bad actions, to accuse us of them; and our good angel, who writes down our good ones, to justify us at the Day of Judgment. When all our actions shall be brought before us, how few will be pleasing to God, even among the best of them! So many imperfections, 'so many thoughts of self-love, human satisfactions, sensual pleasures, self-complacency, will be found mingled with them all! They appear good, but it is only appearance; like those fruits which seem yellow and ripe because they have been pierced by insects."

We see by these fragments that M. Vianney was one of those contemplatives who do not disdain to soften the austerity of their ideas by simple graces of expression, whether out of compassionate kindness to their disciples, or from the natural attraction felt by those who are good for what is beautiful. He found in beautiful creatures Him who is supremely beautiful; he disdained not the least of them. At peace with all things, and having returned in a manner to the primitive innocence and condition of Eden, when Adam beheld creatures in the divine light, and loved them with fraternal charity, his heart overflowed with love, not only for men, but also for all beings visible and invisible. His words breathed an affectionate sympathy for the whole of creation, which no doubt appeared to him in its original dignity and purity. He looked upon it as a sister, who expressed the same thoughts and the same love as himself in another manner. This is shown in his apostrophe to the little birds. Where other eyes perceived nothing but perishable beauties, he discovered, as with a sort of second-sight, the holy harmony and the eternal relations which connect the physical with the moral order—the mysteries of nature with those of faith. He did the same in the region of history. Ages, events, and men were to him only symbols and allegories, prophecies and their accomplishment.

Nothing could be more beautiful, touching, and pathetic, than the application that he made of the legend of St. Alexis to the Real Presence of our Lord.

At the moment when the mother of St. Alexis recognises her son in the lifeless body of the beggar, who has lived thirty years under the staircase of her palace, she cries out, " O my son, why have I known thee so late !" . . The soul, on quitting this life, will see Him Whom it possessed in the Holy Eucharist; and at the sight of the consolations, of the beauty, of the riches that it has failed to recognise, it also will cry out, " O Jesus! O my God ! why have I known Thee so late !"

The Curé of Ars sometimes made edifying reflections on recent events and circumstances which had made an impression upon himself; and though he did it with reserve, we have in this way gained some valuable information, which would otherwise have been lost.

" Because our Lord does not show Himself in the most Holy Sacrament in all His majesty, you behave without respect in His presence; but, nevertheless, He Himself is there. He is in the midst of you. . . . So, when that good Bishop was here the other day, every body was pushing against him. . . . Ah, if they had known he was a Bishop! . . .

"We give our youth to the devil, and the remains of our life to the good God, who is so good that He deigns to be content with even that; . . . but, happily, every one does not do so. A great lady has been here, of one of the first families in France; she went away this morning. She is scarcely three-and-twenty, and she is rich—very rich indeed. . . . She has offered herself in sacrifice to the good God for the expiation of sins, and for the conversion of sinners. She wears a girdle all armed with iron points; she mortifies herself in a thousand ways; and her parents know nothing of it. She is as white as a sheet of paper. Hers is a beautiful soul, very pleasing to the good God, such as are still to be found now and then in the world, and they prevent the world from coming to an end.

"One day, two Protestant ministers came here, who did not believe in the Real Presence of our Lord. I said to them, 'Do you think that a piece of bread could detach itself, and go, of its own accord, to place itself on the tongue of a person who came near to receive it?' 'No.' 'Then it is not bread.' There was a man who had doubts about the Real Presence, and he said, 'What do we know about it? it is not certain. What is consecration? What happens on the altar at that moment?' But he wished to believe, and he prayed the Blessed Virgin to obtain faith for him. Listen attentively to this. I do not say that this happened somewhere, but I say that it happened to myself. *At the moment when this man came up to receive Holy Communion, the Sacred Host detached Itself from my fingers while I was still a good way off, and went of Itself and placed Itself upon the tongue of that man.*"

We will not undertake to give a consecutive view of the teaching of the Curé of Ars. There was indeed a sort of connection between the parts of it, but it would be impossible to describe the sudden inspirations that burst forth and ran through it like rays of light. His catechisms in general defied analysis; and we should be afraid of disfiguring them by reducing them to the formality of a theological system. We shall therefore confine ourselves to offering to our readers an abridgment of some of the most remarkable discourses.

I.

CATECHISM ON SALVATION.

There are many Christians who do not even know why they are in the world. "O my God, why hast Thou sent me into the world?" "To save your soul." "And why dost Thou wish me to be saved?" "Because I love you."

The good God has created us and sent us into the world because He loves us; He wishes to save us because He loves us. . . . To be saved, we must know, love, and serve God. Oh, what a beautiful life! How good, how great a thing it is to know, to love and serve God! We have nothing else to do in this world. All that we do besides is lost time. We must act only for God, and put our works into His hands. . . . We should say, on awaking, "I desire to do every thing to-day for Thee, O my God! I will submit to all that Thou shalt send me, as coming from Thee. I offer myself as a sacrifice to Thee. But, O God, I can do nothing without Thee. Do Thou help me!"

Oh, how bitterly shall we regret at the hour of death the time we have given to pleasures, to useless conversations, to repose, instead of having employed it in mortification, in prayer, in good works, in thinking of our poor misery, in weeping over our poor sins; then we shall see that we have done nothing for heaven.

Oh, my children, how sad it is! Three-quarters of those who are Christians labour for nothing but to satisfy this corpse, which will soon be buried and corrupted, while they do not give a thought to their poor soul, which must be happy or miserable for all eternity. They have no sense nor reason: it makes one tremble.

Look at that man, who is so active and restless, who makes a noise in the world, who wants to govern every body, who thinks himself of consequence, who seems as if he would like to say to the sun, "Go away, and let me enlighten the world instead of you." . . . Some day this proud man will be reduced at the utmost to a little handful of dust, which will be swept away from river to river, from Saône to Saône, and at last into the sea.

See, my children, I often think that we are like those little heaps of sand that the wind raises on the road, which whirl round for a moment, and are scattered directly. . . .

We have brothers and sisters, who are dead. Well, they are reduced to that little handful of dust of which I was speaking.

Worldly people say, it is too difficult to save one's soul. Yet nothing is easier. To observe the commandments of God and the Church, and to avoid the seven capital sins; or if you like to put it so, to do good and avoid evil: that is all.

Good Christians, who labour to save their souls and to work out their salvation, are always happy and contented; they enjoy beforehand the happiness of heaven: they will be happy for all eternity. While bad Christians, who lose their souls, are always to be pitied; they murmur, they are sad, they are as miserable as stones; and they will be so for all eternity. See what a difference!

This is a good rule of conduct, to do nothing but what we can offer to the good God. Now, we cannot offer to Him slanders, calumnies, injustice, anger, blasphemy, impurity, theatres, dancing: yet that is all that people do in the world. Speaking of dances, St. Francis of Sales used to say "that they were like mushrooms, the best were good for nothing." Mothers are apt to say indeed, "Oh, I watch over my daughters." They watch over their toilets, but they cannot watch over their hearts. Those who have dances in their houses load themselves with a terrible responsibility before God; they are answerable for all the evil that is done—for the bad thoughts, the slanders, the jealousies, the hatred, the revenge. . . . Ah, if they well understood this responsibility, they would never have any dances. Just like those who make bad pictures and statues, or write bad books, they will have to answer for all the harm that these things will do during all the time they last. . . . Oh, that makes one tremble!

See, my children, we must reflect that we have a soul to save, and an eternity that awaits us. The world, its riches, pleasures, and honours will pass away; heaven and hell will never pass away. Let us take care, then. The saints did not all begin well; but they all ended well. We have begun badly; let us end well, and we shall go one day and meet them in heaven.

II.

CATECHISM ON THE LOVE OF GOD.

OUR body is a vessel of corruption; it is meant for death and for the worms, nothing more! And yet we devote ourselves to satisfying it, rather than to enriching our soul, which is so great that we can conceive nothing greater—no, nothing, nothing! For we see that God, urged by the ardour of His charity, would not create us like the animals; He has created us in His own image and likeness, do you see? . . . Oh, how great is man!

Man, being created by love, cannot live without love: either he loves God, or he loves himself and he loves the world. See, my children, it is faith that we want. . . . When we have not faith, we are blind. He who does not see, does not know; he who does not know, does not love; he who does not love God loves himself, and at the same time loves his pleasures. He fixes his heart on things which pass away like smoke. He cannot know the truth, nor any good thing; he can know nothing but falsehood, because he has no light; he is in a mist. If he had light, he would see plainly that all that he loves can give him nothing but eternal death; it is a foretaste of hell.

Do you see, my children, except God, nothing is solid—nothing, nothing! If it is life, it passes away; if it is fortune, it crumbles away; if it is health, it is destroyed; if it is reputation, it is attacked. We are scattered like the wind. . . . Every thing is passing away full speed, every thing is going to ruin. O God! O God! how much those are to be pitied, then, who set their hearts on all these things! They set their hearts on them because they love themselves too much; but they do not love themselves with a reasonable love,—they love themselves with a love that seeks themselves and the world, seeking creatures more than God. That is the reason why they are never satisfied, never quiet; they are always uneasy, always tormented, always upset.

See, my children, the good Christian runs his course in this world, mounted on a fine triumphal chariot; this chariot is borne by angels, and conducted by our Lord Himself: while the poor sinner is harnessed to the chariot of this life, and the devil who drives it forces him to go on with great strokes of the whip.

My children, the three acts of faith, hope, and charity contain all the happiness of man upon the earth. By faith, we believe what God has promised us: we believe that we shall one day see Him, that we shall possess Him, that we shall be eternally happy with Him in heaven. By hope, we expect the fulfilment of these promises: we hope that we shall be rewarded for all our good actions, for all our good thoughts, for all our good desires; for God takes into account even our good desires. What more do we want to make us happy?

In heaven, faith and hope will exist no more, for the mists which obscure our reason will be dispelled; our mind will be able to understand the things that are hidden from it here below. We shall no longer hope for any thing, because we shall have every thing. We do not hope to acquire a treasure which we already possess.... But love! oh, we shall be inebriated with it! we shall be drowned, lost in that ocean of divine love, annihilated in that immense charity of the Heart of Jesus! so that charity is a foretaste of heaven. Oh! how happy should we be if we knew how to understand it, to feel it, to taste it! What makes us unhappy is, that we do not love God.

When we say, "My God, I believe, I believe firmly, that is, without the least doubt, without the least hesitation"... Oh, if we were penetrated with these words: "I firmly believe that Thou art present every where, that Thou seest me, that I am under Thine eyes; that one day I myself shall see Thee clearly, that I shall enjoy all the good things Thou hast promised me! O my God, I hope that Thou wilt reward me for all that I have done to please Thee! O my God, I love Thee; my heart is made to love Thee!" Oh, this act of faith, which is also an act of love, would suffice for every thing! If we understood our own happiness in being able to love God, we should remain motionless in ecstasy....

If a prince, an emperor were to cause one of his subjects to appear before him, and should say to him, "I wish to make you happy; stay with me, enjoy all my possessions, but be careful not to give me any just cause of displeasure," with what care, with what ardour, would not that subject endeavour to satisfy his prince! Well, God makes the same proposals to us, . . . and we do not care for His friendship, we make no account of His promises. . . . What a pity!

III.

CATECHISM ON THE PREROGATIVES OF THE PURE SOUL.

Nothing is so beautiful as a pure soul. If we understood this, we could not lose our purity. The pure soul is disengaged from matter, from earthly things, and from itself. . . . That is why the saints ill-treated their body, that is why they did not grant it what it required, not even to rise five minutes later, to warm themselves, to eat any thing that gave them pleasure. . . . For what the body loses the soul gains, and what the body gains the soul loses.

Purity comes from heaven; we must ask for

it from God. If we ask for it, we shall obtain it. We must take great care not to lose it. We must shut our heart against pride, against sensuality, and all the other passions, as one shuts the doors and windows that nobody may be able to get in.

What joy is it to the guardian angel to conduct a pure soul! My children, when a soul is pure, all heaven looks upon it with love!

Pure souls will form the circle round our Lord. The more pure we have been on earth, the nearer we shall be to Him in heaven.

When the heart is pure, it cannot help loving, because it has found the Source of love, which is God. "Happy," says our Lord, "are the pure in heart, because they shall see God!"

My children, we cannot comprehend the power that a pure soul has over the good God. It is not he who does the will of God, it is God Who does his will. Look at Moses, that very pure soul. When God would punish the Jewish people, He said to him, Do not pray for them, because My anger must fall upon this people. Nevertheless, Moses prayed, and God spared His people; He let Himself be entreated; He could not resist the prayer of that pure soul. O my children, a soul that has never been stained by that accursed sin obtains from God whatever it wishes!

Three things are wanted to preserve purity—the presence of God, prayer, and the Sacraments. Another means is the reading of holy books, which nourishes the soul.

How beautiful is a pure soul! Our Lord showed one to St. Catherine; she thought it so beautiful that she said, "O Lord, if I did not know that there is only one God, I should think it was one." The image of God is reflected in a pure soul, like the sun in the water.

A pure soul is the admiration of the Three Persons of the Holy Trinity. The Father contemplates His work: There is My creature! . . . The Son, the price of His Blood: the beauty of an object is shown by the price it has cost. . . . The Holy Spirit dwells in it, as in a temple.

We also know the value of our soul by the efforts the devil makes to ruin it. Hell is leagued against it—heaven for it. . . . Oh, how great it must be!

In order to have an idea of our dignity, we must often think of heaven, Calvary, and hell. If we could understand what it is to be the child of God, we could not do evil,—we should be like angels on earth. To be children of God, oh, what a dignity!

It is a beautiful thing to have a heart, and, little as it is, to be able to make use of it in loving God. How shameful it is that man should descend so low, when God has placed him so high!

When the angels had revolted against God, this God who is so good, seeing that they could no longer enjoy the happiness for which He had created them, made man, and this little world that we see to nourish his body. But his soul required to be nourished also; and as nothing created can feed the soul, which is a spirit, God willed to give Himself for its food.

But the great misfortune is, that we neglect to have recourse to this divine food, in crossing the desert of this life. Like people who die of hunger within sight of a well-provided table, there are some who remain fifty, sixty years, without feeding their souls.

Oh, if Christians could understand the language of our Lord, who says to them, "Notwithstanding thy misery, I wish to see near Me that beautiful soul which I created for Myself. I made it so great, that nothing can fill it but Myself. I made it so pure, that nothing but My Body can nourish it."

Our Lord has always distinguished pure souls. Look at St. John, the well-beloved disciple, who reposed upon His breast. . . ! St. Catherine was pure, and she was often transported into Paradise. When she died, angels took up her body, and carried it to Mount Sinai, where Moses had received the Commandments of the law. God has shown by this prodigy that a soul is so agreeable to Him that it deserves that even the body which has participated in its purity should be buried by angels.

God contemplates a pure soul with love; He grants it all it desires. How could He refuse any thing to a soul that lives only for Him, by Him, and in Him? It seeks Him, and God shows Himself to it; it calls Him, and God comes; it is one with Him; it captivates His will. A pure soul is all-powerful with the gracious Heart of our Lord.

A pure soul with God is like a child with its mother. It caresses her, it embraces her, and its mother returns its caresses and embraces.

IV.

CATECHISM ON THE HOLY SPIRIT.

O MY children, how beautiful it is! The Father is our Creator, the Son is our Redeemer, and the Holy Ghost is our Guide...

Man by himself is nothing, but with the

Holy Spirit he is very great. Man is all earthly, and all animal; nothing but the Holy Spirit can elevate his mind, and raise it on high. Why were the saints so detached from the earth? Because they let themselves be led by the Holy Spirit. Those who are led by the Holy Spirit have true ideas; that is the reason that so many ignorant people are wiser than the learned. When we are led by a God of strength and light, we cannot go astray.

The Holy Spirit is light and strength. He teaches us to distinguish between truth and falsehood, and between good and evil. Like glasses that magnify objects, the Holy Spirit shows us good and evil on a large scale. With the Holy Spirit we see every thing in its true proportions; we see the greatness of the least actions done for God, and the greatness of the least faults. As a watchmaker with his glasses distinguishes the most minute wheels of a watch, so we, with the light of the Holy Ghost, distinguish all the details of our poor life. Then the smallest imperfections appear very great, the least sins inspire us with horror. That is the reason why the most Holy Virgin never sinned. The Holy Ghost made her understand the hideousness of sin; she shuddered with terror at the least fault.

Those who have the Holy Spirit cannot endure themselves, so well do they know their poor misery. The proud are those who have not the Holy Spirit.

Worldly people have not the Holy Spirit, or if they have, it is only for a moment. He does not remain with them; the noise of the world drives Him away. A Christian who is led by the Holy Spirit has no difficulty in leaving the goods of this world, to run after those of heaven; he knows the difference between them. The eyes of the world see no farther than this life, as mine see no farther than this wall when the church-door is shut. The eyes of the Christian see deep into eternity. To the man who gives himself up to the guidance of the Holy Ghost, there seems to be no world ; to the world there seems to be no God. . . . We must therefore find out by whom we are led. If it is not by the Holy Ghost, we labour in vain, there is no substance nor savour in any thing we do. If it is by the Holy Ghost, we taste a delicious sweetness; . . . it is enough to make us die of pleasure!

Those who are led by the Holy Spirit experience all sorts of happiness in themselves, while bad Christians roll themselves on thorns and flints.

A soul in which the Holy Spirit dwells is

never weary in the presence of God; his heart gives forth a breath of love.

Without the Holy Ghost we are like the stones on the road. . . . Take in one hand a sponge full of water, and in the other a little pebble; press them equally. Nothing will come out of the pebble, but out of the sponge will come abundance of water. The sponge is the soul filled with the Holy Spirit, and the stone is the cold and hard heart which is not inhabited by the Holy Spirit.

A soul that possesses the Holy Spirit tastes such sweetness in prayer, that she finds the time always too short; she never loses the holy presence of God. Such a heart, before our good Saviour in the Holy Sacrament of the Altar, is a bunch of grapes under the wine-press.

The Holy Spirit forms thoughts and suggests words in the hearts of the just. . . . Those who have the Holy Spirit produce nothing bad: all the fruits of the Holy Spirit are good.

Without the Holy Spirit all is cold; therefore, when we feel we are losing our fervour, we must instantly make a novena to the Holy Spirit to ask for faith and love. . . . See, when we have made a retreat or a jubilee, we are full of good desires: these good desires are the breath of the Holy Ghost, which has passed over our souls, and has renewed every thing, like the warm wind which melts the ice and brings back the spring. . . . You who are not great saints, you still have many moments when you taste the sweetness of prayer and of the presence of God: these are visits of the Holy Spirit. When we have the Holy Spirit, the heart expands—bathes itself in divine love. A fish never complains of having too much water, neither does a good Christian ever complain of being too long with the good God. There are some people who find religion wearisome, and it is because they have not the Holy Spirit.

If the damned were asked, Why are you in hell? they would answer, For having resisted the Holy Spirit. And if the saints were asked, Why are you in heaven? they would answer, For having listened to the Holy Spirit. When good thoughts come into our minds, it is the Holy Spirit who is visiting us.

The Holy Spirit is a power. The Holy Spirit supported St. Simeon on his column; He sustained the martyrs. Without the Holy Spirit, the martyrs would have fallen like the leaves from the trees. When the fires were lighted under them, the Holy Spirit extinguished the heat of the fire by the heat of divine love.

The good God, in sending us the Holy Spirit, has treated us like a great king who should send his minister to guide one of his subjects, saying, "You will accompany this man every where, and you will bring him back to me safe and sound." How beautiful it is, my children, to be accompanied by the Holy Spirit! He is indeed a good Guide; and to think that there are some who will not follow Him!

The Holy Spirit is like a man with a carriage and horse, who should want to take us to Paris. We should only have to say 'yes,' and to get into it. It is indeed an easy matter to say yes! . . . Well, the Holy Spirit wants to take us to heaven; we have only to say 'yes,' and to let Him take us there.

The Holy Spirit is like a gardener cultivating our souls. . . . The Holy Spirit is our servant. . . .

There is a gun; well, you load it, but some one must fire it and make it go off. . . . In the same way, we have in ourselves the power of doing good; . . . when the Holy Spirit gives the impulse, good works are produced.

The Holy Spirit reposes in just souls like the dove in her nest. He brings out good desires in a pure soul, as the dove hatches her young ones.

The Holy Spirit leads us as a mother leads by the hand her child of two years old, . . . as a person who can see leads one who is blind.

The Sacraments which our Lord instituted would not have saved us without the Holy Spirit. Even the Death of our Lord would have been useless to us without Him. Therefore our Lord said to His Apostles, "It is good for you that I should go away; for if I did not go, the Consoler would not come." . . . The descent of the Holy Ghost was required, to render fruitful that harvest of graces. It is like a grain of wheat—you cast it into the ground; yes, but it must have sun and rain to make it grow and come into ear.

We should say every morning, "O God, send me Thy Spirit, to teach me what I am and what Thou art."

V.

CATECHISM ON THE BLESSED VIRGIN.

The Father takes pleasure in looking upon the heart of the most Holy Virgin Mary, as the masterpiece of His hands; for we always like our own work, especially when it is well done. The Son takes pleasure in it as the heart of

His Mother, the source from which He drew the Blood that has ransomed us; the Holy Ghost as His temple.

The Prophets published the glory of Mary before her birth; they compared her to the sun. Indeed, the apparition of the Holy Virgin may well be compared to a beautiful gleam of sun on a foggy day.

Before her coming, the anger of God was hanging over our heads like a sword ready to strike us. As soon as the Holy Virgin appeared upon the earth, His anger was appeased. . . . She did not know that she was to be the Mother of God, and when she was a little child she used to say, "When shall I then see that beautiful creature who is to be the Mother of God?"

The Holy Virgin has brought us forth twice, in the Incarnation and at the foot of the Cross; she is then doubly our Mother.

The Holy Virgin is often compared to a mother, but she is much better still than the best of mothers; for the best of mothers sometimes punishes her child when it displeases her, and even beats it: she thinks she is doing right. But the Holy Virgin does not so; she is so good that she treats us with love, and never punishes us.

The heart of this good Mother is all love and

mercy; she desires only to see us happy. We have only to turn to her to be heard.

The Son has His justice, the Mother has nothing but her love.

God has loved us so much as to die for us; but in the heart of our Lord there is justice, which is an attribute of God; in that of the most Holy Virgin there is nothing but mercy. Her Son was ready to punish a sinner; Mary interposes, checks the sword, implores pardon for the poor criminal. "Mother," our Lord says to her, "I can refuse you nothing. If hell could repent, you would obtain its pardon."

The most Holy Virgin places herself between her Son and us. The greater sinners we are, the more tenderness and compassion does she feel for us. The child that has cost its mother most tears is the dearest to her heart. Does not a mother always run to the help of the weakest and the most exposed to danger? Is not a physician in the hospital most attentive to those who are most seriously ill?

The Heart of Mary is so tender towards us, that those of all the mothers in the world put together are like a piece of ice in comparison to hers.

See how good the Holy Virgin is! Her great servant St. Bernard used often to say to her, "I salute thee, Mary." . . . One day this good

Mother answered him, "I salute thee, my son Bernard." . . .

The *Ave Maria* is a prayer that is never wearisome.

The devotion to the Holy Virgin is delicious, sweet, nourishing. When we talk on earthly subjects or politics, we grow weary; but when we talk of the Holy Virgin, it is always new.

All the saints have a great devotion to our Lady; no grace comes from heaven without passing through her hands. We cannot go into a house without speaking to the porter; well, the Holy Virgin is the portress of heaven.

When we have to offer any thing to a great personage, we get it presented by the person he likes best, in order that the homage may be agreeable to him. So our prayers have quite a different sort of merit when they are presented by the Blessed Virgin, because she is the only creature who has never offended God. The Blessed Virgin alone has fulfilled the first commandment — to adore God only, and love Him perfectly. She fulfilled it completely.

All that the Son asks of the Father is granted Him. All that the Mother asks of the Son is in like manner granted to her.

When we have handled something fragrant,

our hands perfume whatever they touch: let our prayer pass through the hands of the Holy Virgin; she will perfume them.

I think that at the end of the world the Blessed Virgin will be very tranquil; but while the world lasts, we drag her in all directions. . . . The Holy Virgin is like a mother who has a great many children,—she is continually occupied in going from one to the other.

VI.

CATECHISM ON THE SANCTIFICATION OF SUNDAY.

You labour, you labour, my children; but what you earn ruins your body and your soul. If one asked those who work on Sunday, "What have you been doing?" they might answer, "I have been selling my soul to the devil, crucifying our Lord, and renouncing my Baptism. I am going to hell; I shall have to weep for all eternity in vain." When I see people driving carts on Sunday, I think I see them carrying their souls to hell.

Oh, how mistaken in his calculations is he who labours hard on Sunday, thinking that he will earn more money or do more work! Can two or three shillings ever make up for the harm he does himself by violating the law of the good God? You imagine that every thing depends on your working; but there comes an illness, an accident . . . so little is required! a tempest, a hailstorm, a frost. The good God holds every thing in His hand; He can avenge Himself when He will, and as He will; the means are not wanting to Him. Is He not always the strongest? Must not He be the master in the end?

There was once a woman who came to her priest to ask leave to get in her hay on Sunday. "But," said the priest, "it is not necessary; your hay will run no risk." This woman insisted, saying, "Then you want me to let my crop be lost?" She herself died that very evening; . . . she was more in danger than her crop of hay. . . .

"Labour not for the meat which perisheth, but for that which endureth unto life everlasting."*

What will remain to you of your Sunday work? You leave the earth just as it is; when you go away, you carry nothing with you. Ah! when we are attached to the earth, we are not willing to go! . . . Our first aim is to go to God; we are on the earth for no other purpose,

* St. John vi. 27.

My brethren, we should die on Sunday, and rise again on Monday.

Sunday is the property of our good God; it is His own day, the Lord's day. He made all the days of the week: He might have kept them all; He has given you six, and has reserved only the seventh for Himself. What right have you to meddle with what does not belong to you? You know very well that stolen goods never bring any profit. Nor will the day that you steal from our Lord profit you either. I know two very certain ways of becoming poor: they are, working on Sunday, and taking other people's property.

VII.

CATECHISM ON THE WORD OF GOD.

My children, the Word of God is of no little importance! These were our Lord's first words to His Apostles, "Go and teach,"... to show us that instruction is before every thing.

My children, what has taught us our religion?—The instructions we have heard. What gives us a horror of sin?... what makes us alive to the beauty of virtue, . . . inspires us with the desire of heaven?—Instructions. What teaches fathers and mothers the duties they have to fulfil towards their children, and children the duties they have to fulfil towards their parents?—Instructions.

My children, why are people so blind and so ignorant? Because they make so little account of the Word of God. There are some who do not even say a *Pater* and an *Ave* to beg of the good God the grace to listen to it attentively, and to profit well by it. I believe, my children, that a person who does not hear the Word of God as he ought, will not be saved; he will not know what to do to be saved. But with a well-instructed person there is always some resource. He may wander in all sorts of evil ways; there is still hope that he will return sooner or later to the good God, even if it were only at the hour of death. Instead of which, a person who has never been instructed is like a sick person—like one in his agony who is no longer conscious: he knows neither the greatness of sin nor the value of virtue; he drags himself from sin to sin, like a rag that is dragged in the mud.

See, my children, the esteem in which our Lord holds the word of God; to the woman who cries, "Blessed is the womb that bore

Thee, and the paps that gave Thee suck!" he answers, "Yea, rather blessed are they who hear the Word of God and keep it!"

Our Lord, who is Truth itself, puts no less value on His Word than on His Body. I do not know whether it is worse to have distractions during Mass than during the instructions; I see no difference. During Mass we lose the merits of the Death and Passion of our Lord, and during the instructions we lose His Word, which is Himself. St. Augustine says that it is as bad as to take the chalice after the consecration and to trample it under foot.

My children, you make a scruple of missing holy Mass, because you commit a great sin in missing it by your own fault; but you have no scruple in missing an instruction. You never consider that in this way you may greatly offend God. At the Day of Judgment, when you will all be there around me, and the good God will say to you, "Give Me an account of the instructions and the catechisms which you have heard and which you might have heard," . . . you will think very differently. My children, you go out during the instructions, you amuse yourselves with laughing, you do not listen, you think yourselves too clever to come to the catechism; . . . do you think, my children, that things will be allowed to go on so? Oh, no, certainly not! God will arrange matters very differently.

How sad it is! We see fathers and mothers stay outside during the instructions; yet they are under obligations to instruct their children; but how can they teach them? They are not instructed themselves. . . . All this leads straight to hell. . . . It is a pity!

My children, I have remarked that there is no moment when people are more inclined to sleep than during the instructions. . . . You will say, I am so very sleepy. . . . If I were to take up a fiddle, nobody would think of sleeping; every body would be roused, every body would be on the alert. My children, you listen when you like the preacher; but if the preacher does not suit you, you turn him into ridicule. . . . We must not think so much about the man. It is not the body that we must attend to. Whatever the priest may be, he is still the instrument that the good God makes use of to distribute His holy Word. You pour liquor through a funnel; whether it be made of gold or of copper, if the liquor is good it will still be good.

There are some who go about repeating every where, "Priests say just what they please." No, my children, priests do not say what they please; they say what is in the Gospel. The priests who came before us said what we say; those who shall come after us will say the same thing. If we were to say things that were not true, the Bishop would very soon forbid us to preach. We say only what our Lord has taught.

My children, I will give you an example of what it is not to believe what priests tell you. There were two soldiers passing through a place where a mission was being given; one of the soldiers proposed to his comrade to go and hear the sermon, and they went. The missionary preached upon hell. "Do you believe all that this priest says?" asked the least wicked of the two. "Oh, no!" replied the other, "I believe it is all nonsense, invented to frighten people." "Well, for my part, I believe it; and to prove to you that I believe it, I shall give up being a soldier, and go into a convent." "Go where you please; I shall continue my journey." But while he was on his journey, he fell ill and died. The other, who was in the convent, heard of his death, and began to pray that God would show him in what state his companion had died. One day, as he was praying, this companion appeared to him; he recognised him, and asked him, "Where are you?" "In hell; I am lost!" "O wretched man! do you now believe what the missionary said?" "Yes, I believe it. Missionaries are wrong only in one respect; they do not tell you a hundredth part of what is suffered here."

My children, I often think that most of the Christians who are lost are lost for want of instruction—they do not know their religion well. For example, here is a person who has to go and do his day's work. This person has a desire to do great penances, to pass half the night in prayer; if he is well instructed, he will say, "No, I must not do that, because then I could not fulfil my duty to-morrow; I should be sleepy, and the least thing would put me out of patience; I should be weary all the day, and I should not do half as much work as if I had rested at night; that must not be done." Again, my children, a servant may have a desire to fast, but he is obliged to pass the whole day in digging or ploughing, or whatever you please. Well, if this servant is well instructed, he will think, "But if I do this, I shall not be able to satisfy my master." Well, what will he do? He will eat his breakfast, and mortify himself in some other way. That is what we must do—we must always act in the way that will give most glory to the good God.

A person knows that another is in distress, and takes from his parents what will relieve that distress. He would certainly do much better to ask than to take it. If his parents refuse to give it, he will pray to God to inspire a rich person to give the alms instead of him.

A well-instructed person always has two guides leading the way before him—good counsel and obedience.

VIII.

CATECHISM ON PRAYER.

SEE, my children; the treasure of a Christian is not on the earth, it is in heaven. Well, our thoughts ought to be where our treasure is.

Man has a beautiful office, that of praying and loving. . . . You pray, you love—that is the happiness of man upon the earth.

Prayer is nothing else than union with God. When our heart is pure and united to God, we feel within ourselves a joy, a sweetness that inebriates, a light that dazzles us. In this intimate union God and the soul are like two pieces of wax melted together; they cannot be separated. This union of God with His little creature is a most beautiful thing. It is a happiness that we cannot understand.

We have not deserved to pray; but God, in His goodness, has permitted us to speak to Him.

Our prayer is an incense which He receives with extreme pleasure.

My children, your heart is poor and narrow; but prayer enlarges it, and renders it capable of loving God. Prayer is a foretaste of heaven, an overflow of paradise. It never leaves us without sweetness. It is like honey descending into the soul and sweetening every thing. Troubles melt away before a fervent prayer like snow before the sun.

Prayer makes time pass very quickly, and so pleasantly that one does not perceive how it passes. Do you know, when I was running up and down the country, at the time that almost all the poor priests were ill, I was praying to the good God all along the road? I assure you, the time did not seem long to me.

We see some persons who lose themselves in prayer like a fish in the water, because they are all for God. There is no division in their heart. Oh, how I love those generous souls! St. Francis of Assisi and St. Colette saw our Lord and spoke to Him as we talk to each other. While we, how often we come to church without knowing what we come for, or what we are going to ask! And yet, when we go to any one's house, we know very well what we are going for. . . . Some people seem to say to God, "I am going to say two words to Thee, to get rid of Thee." I often think that when we come to adore our Lord, we should obtain all we wish, if we would ask it with very lively faith and a very pure heart. But, alas! we have no faith, no hope, no desire, no love!

There are two cries in man, the cry of the angel and the cry of the beast. The cry of the angel is prayer; the cry of the beast is sin. Those who do not pray, stoop towards the earth, like a mole trying to make a hole to hide itself in. They are all earthly, all brutish, and think of nothing but temporal things, . . . like that miser who was receiving the last Sacraments the other day; when they gave him a silver crucifix to kiss, he said, " That cross weighs full ten ounces."

If there could be one day without worship in heaven, it would no longer be heaven; and if the poor lost souls, notwithstanding their sufferings, could worship, there would be no more hell. Alas! they had a heart to love God with, a tongue to bless Him with; that was their destiny. And now they are condemned to curse Him through all eternity. If they could hope that they would once pray only for one minute, they would watch for that minute with such impatience that it would lessen their torments.

"Our Father who art in heaven!" . . . Oh, how beautiful it is, my children, to have a Father in heaven! "Thy kingdom come." . . . If I make the good God reign in my heart, He will make me reign with Him in His glory. "Thy will be done." There is nothing so sweet, and nothing so perfect, as to do the will of God. In order to do things well, we must do them as God wills, in all conformity with His designs. "Give us this day our daily bread." We are composed of two parts, the soul and the body. We ask the good God to feed our poor body, and He answers by making the earth produce all that is necessary for our support. . . . . But we ask Him to feed our soul, which is the best part of ourselves; and the earth is too small to furnish enough to satisfy it; it hungers for God, and nothing but God can satiate it. Therefore, the good God thought He did not do too much, in dwelling upon the earth and assuming a body, in order that this Body might become the food of our souls. "My Flesh," said our Lord, "is meat indeed. . . . The bread that I will give is My Flesh, for the life of the world."

The bread of souls is in the tabernacle. The tabernacle is the storehouse of Christians. . . .

Oh, how beautiful it is, my children! When the priest presents the Host, and shows it to you, your soul may say, There is my food. O my children, we are too happy! ... We shall never comprehend it till we are in heaven. What a pity that is!

IX.

CATECHISM ON THE PRIESTHOOD.

My children, we have come to the Sacrament of Orders. It is a Sacrament which seems to relate to no one among you, and which yet relates to every one. This Sacrament raises man up to God. What is a priest? A man who holds the place of God—a man who is invested with all the powers of God. "Go," said our Lord to the priest; "as my Father sent Me, I send you. All power has been given Me in heaven and on earth. Go then, teach all nations. ... He who listens to you, listens to Me; he who despises you, despises Me."

When the priest remits sins, he does not say, "God pardons you;" he says, "I absolve you." At the Consecration, he does not say, "This is the Body of our Lord;" he says, "This is My Body."

St. Bernard tells us that every thing has come to us through Mary; and we may also say that every thing has come to us through the priest; yes, all happiness, all graces, all heavenly gifts.

If we had not the Sacrament of Orders, we should not have our Lord. Who placed Him there, in that tabernacle? It was the priest. Who was it that received your soul, on its entrance into life? The priest. Who nourishes it, to give it strength to make its pilgrimage? The priest. Who will prepare it to appear before God, by washing that soul, for the last time, in the Blood of Jesus Christ? The priest—always the priest. And if that soul comes to the point of death, who will raise it up, who will restore it to calmness and peace? Again, the priest. You cannot recall one single blessing from God without finding, side by side with this recollection, the image of the priest.

Go to confession to the Blessed Virgin, or to an angel; will they absolve you? No. Will they give you the Body and Blood of our Lord? No. The Holy Virgin cannot make her Divine Son descend into the Host. You might have two hundred angels there, but they could not absolve you. A priest, however simple he may be, can do it; he can say to you, " Go in

Oh, how great is a priest! The priest will not understand the greatness of his office till he is in heaven. If he understood it on earth, he would die, not of fear, but of love.

The other benefits of God would be of no avail to us without the priest. What would be the use of a house full of gold, if you had nobody to open you the door? The priest has the key of the heavenly treasures; it is he who opens the door; he is the steward of the good God, the distributor of His wealth.

Without the priest, the Death and Passion of our Lord would be of no avail. Look at the heathens: what has it availed them that our Lord has died? Alas! they can have no share in the blessings of redemption, while they have no priests to apply His Blood to their souls!

The priest is not a priest for himself; he does not give himself absolution; he does not administer the Sacraments to himself. He is not for himself, he is for you.

After God, the priest is every thing. Leave a parish twenty years without priests; they will worship beasts.

If the Missionary Father and I were to go away, you would say, "What can we do in this church? there is no Mass; our Lord is no longer there: we may as well pray at home."

When people wish to destroy religion, they begin by attacking the priest, because where there is no longer any priest there is no sacrifice, and where there is no longer any sacrifice there is no religion.

When the bell calls you to church, if you were asked, " Where are you going?" you might answer, " I am going to feed my soul." If some one were to ask you, pointing to the tabernacle, " What is that golden door?" " That is our storehouse, where the true Food of our souls is kept.' " Who has the key? Who lays in the provisions? Who makes ready the feast, and who serves the table?" " The priest." " And what is the Food?" " The precious Body and Blood of our Lord." O God! O God! how Thou hast loved us! . . .

See the power of the priest; out of a piece of bread the word of a priest makes a God. It is more than creating the world. . . . Some one said, " Does St. Philomena, then, obey the Curé of Ars?" Indeed, she may well obey him, since God obeys him.

If I were to meet a priest and an angel, I should salute the priest before I saluted the angel. The latter is the friend of God; but the priest holds His place. St. Teresa kissed the ground where a priest had passed. When you see a priest, you should say, " There is he who made me a child of God, and opened heaven to me by holy Baptism; he who purified me after I had sinned; who gives nourishment to my soul." At the sight of a church-tower, you may say, "What is there in that place?" "The Body of our Lord." "Why is He there?" "Because a priest has been there, and has said holy Mass."

What joy did the Apostles feel after the Resurrection of our Lord, at seeing the Master whom they had loved so much! The priest must feel the same joy, at seeing our Lord whom he holds in his hands. Great value is attached to objects which have been laid in the drinking-cup of the Blessed Virgin and of the Child Jesus, at Loretto. But the fingers of the priest, that have touched the adorable Flesh of Jesus Christ, that have been plunged into the chalice which contained His Blood, into the pyx where His Body has lain, are they not still more precious?

The priesthood is the love of the Heart of Jesus. When you see the priest, think of our Lord Jesus Christ.

X.

CATECHISM ON THE HOLY SACRIFICE OF THE MASS.

ALL good works together are not of equal value with the sacrifice of the Mass, because they are the works of men, and the holy Mass is the work of God. Martyrdom is nothing in comparison ; it is the sacrifice that man makes of his life to God; the Mass is the sacrifice that God makes to man of His Body and of His Blood. Oh, how great is a priest! if he understood himself, he would die.... God obeys him; he speaks two words, and our Lord comes down from heaven at his voice, and shuts himself up in a little Host. God looks upon the Altar. "That is My well-beloved Son," He says, "in Whom I am well pleased."

He can refuse nothing to the merits of the offering of this Victim. If we had faith, we should see God hidden in the priest like a light behind a glass, like wine mingled with water.

After the Consecration, when I hold in my hands the most holy Body of our Lord, and when I am in discouragement, seeing myself worthy of nothing but hell, I say to myself, "Ah, if I could at least take Him with me! Hell would be sweet with Him; I could be content to remain suffering there for all eternity, if we were together. But then there would be no more hell; the flames of love would extinguish those of justice."

How beautiful it is! After the Consecration, the good God is there as He is in heaven. If man well understood this mystery, he would die of love. God spares us because of our weakness.

A priest once, after the Consecration, had some little doubt whether his few words could have made our Lord descend upon the Altar; at the same moment he saw the Host all red, and the corporal tinged with blood.

If some one said to us, " At such an hour a dead person is to be raised to life," we should run very quickly to see it. But is not the Consecration which changes bread and wine into the Body and Blood of God, a much greater miracle than to raise a dead person to life? We ought always to devote at least a quarter of an hour to preparing ourselves to hear Mass well; we ought to annihilate ourselves before God, after the example of His profound annihilation in the Sacrament of the Eucharist; and we should make our examination of conscience, for we must be in a state of grace to be able to assist properly at Mass.

If we knew the value of the holy Sacrifice of the Mass, or rather if we had faith, we should be much more zealous to assist at it.

My children, you remember the story I have told you already of that holy priest who was praying for his friend; God had, it appears, made known to him that he was in purgatory; it came into his mind that he could do nothing better than to offer the holy Sacrifice of the Mass for his soul. When he came to the moment of Consecration, he took the Host in his hands and said, "O Holy and Eternal Father, let us make an exchange. Thou hast the soul of my friend who is in purgatory, and I have the Body of Thy Son, who is in my hands; well, do Thou deliver my friend, and I offer Thee Thy Son, with all the merits of His Death and Passion." In fact, at the moment of the elevation, he saw the soul of his friend rising to heaven, all radiant with glory. Well, my children, when we want to obtain any thing from the good God, let us do the same; after Holy Communion, let us offer Him His well-beloved Son, with all the merits of His Death and His Passion. He will not be able to refuse us any thing.

XI.

CATECHISM ON THE REAL PRESENCE.

Our Lord is hidden there, waiting for us to come and visit Him, and make our requests to Him. See how good He is! He accommodates Himself to our weakness. In heaven, where we shall be glorious and triumphant, we shall see Him in all His glory. If He had presented Himself before us in that glory now, we should not have dared to approach Him; but He hides Himself, like a person in a prison, who might say to us, "You do not see me, but that is no matter; ask of me all you wish, and I will grant it. He is there in the Sacrament of His love, sighing and interceding incessantly with His Father for sinners. To what outrages does He not expose Himself, that He may remain in the midst of us! He is there to console us; and therefore we ought often to visit Him. How pleasing to Him is the short quarter of an hour that we steal from our occupations, from something of no use, to come and pray to Him, to visit Him, to console Him for all the outrages He receives! When He sees pure souls coming eagerly to Him, He smiles upon them. . . . They come with that simplicity which pleases Him so much, to ask His pardon for all sinners, for the outrages of so many ungrateful men. What happiness do we not find in the presence of God, when we find ourselves alone at His feet before the holy tabernacles! "Come, my soul, redouble thy fervour; thou art alone adoring thy God. His eyes rest upon thee alone." This good Saviour is so full of love for us, that He seeks us out every where.

Ah! if we had the eyes of angels with which to see our Lord Jesus Christ, Who is here present on this Altar, and Who is looking at us, how we should love Him! We should never more wish to part from Him; we should wish to remain always at His feet; it would be a foretaste of heaven: all else would become insipid to us. But see, it is faith we want. We are poor blind people; we have a mist before our eyes. Faith alone can dispel this mist. Presently, my children, when I shall hold our Lord in my hands, when the good God blesses you, ask Him then to open the eyes of your heart; say to Him, like the blind man of Jericho, "O Lord, make me to see!" If you say to him sincerely, "Make me to see!" you will certainly obtain what you desire, because He wishes nothing but your happiness. He has His hands full of graces, seeking to whom to distribute them; alas! and no one will have them. . . . Oh, indifference! Oh, ingratitude! My children, we are most unhappy that we do not understand these things! We shall understand them well one day; but it will then be too late!

Our Lord is there as a Victim; and a prayer that is very pleasing to God is to ask the Blessed Virgin to offer to the Eternal Father her Divine Son, all bleeding, all torn, for the conversion of sinners; it is the best prayer we can make, since, indeed, all prayers are made in the name and through the merits of Jesus Christ. We must also thank God for all those indulgences that purify us from our sins . . . . but we pay no attention to them. We tread upon indulgences, one might say, as we tread upon the sheaves of corn after the harvest. See, there are seven years and seven quarantines for hearing the Catechism, three hundred days for reciting the Litany of the Blessed Virgin, the Salve Regina, the Angelus. In short, the good God multiplies His graces upon us; and how sorry we shall be at the end of our lives that we did not profit by them!

When we are before the Blessed Sacrament, instead of looking about, let us shut our eyes and our mouth; let us open our heart: our good God will open His; we shall go to Him, He will come to us, the one to ask, the other to receive; it will be like a breath from one to the other. What sweetness do we not find in forgetting ourselves in order to seek God! The saints lost sight of themselves that they might see nothing but God, and labour for Him alone; they forgot all created objects in order to find Him alone. This is the way to reach heaven.

XII.

CATECHISM ON COMMUNION.

When God willed to give nourishment to our soul to sustain it in the pilgrimage of life, He looked over creation, and found nothing that was worthy of it. He then turned to Himself, and resolved to give Himself. . . . O my soul, how great thou art, since nothing less than God can satisfy thee! The Food of the soul is the Body and Blood of God! Oh, admirable Food! If we considered it, it would make us lose ourselves in that abyss of love for all eternity!

How happy are the pure souls that have the happiness of being united to our Lord by communion! They will shine like beautiful diamonds in heaven, because God will be seen in them.*

* "Gloria ejus in te videbitur" (Isaias lx. 2).

Our Lord has said, Whatever you shall ask the Father in My name, He will give it you. We should never have thought of asking of God His own Son. But God has done what man could not have imagined. What man cannot express nor conceive, and what he never would have dared to desire, God in His love has said, has conceived, and has executed. Should we ever have dared to ask of God to put His Son to death for us, to give us His Flesh to eat and His Blood to drink? If all this were not true, then man might have imagined things that God cannot do; he would have gone farther than God in inventions of love! That is impossible.

Without the Holy Eucharist there would be no happiness in this world; life would be insupportable. When we receive Holy Communion, we receive our joy and our happiness.

The good God, wishing to give Himself to us in the Sacrament of His love, gave us a vast and great desire, which He alone can satisfy. In the presence of this beautiful Sacrament, we are like a person dying of thirst by the side of a river—he would only need to bend his head; . . . like a person still remaining poor close to a great treasure—he need only stretch out his hand.

He who communicates loses himself in God

like a drop of water in the ocean. They can no more be separated.

At the Day of Judgment we shall see the Flesh of our Lord shine through the glorified body of those who have received Him worthily on earth, as we see gold shine in copper, or silver in lead.

When we have just communicated, if we were asked, "What are you carrying away to your home?" we might answer, "I am carrying away heaven." A saint said that we were Christ-bearers. It is very true; but we have not enough faith. We do not comprehend our dignity. When we leave the holy banquet, we are as happy as the Wise Men would have been if they could have carried away the Infant Jesus.

Take a vessel full of liquor, and cork it well; you will keep the liquor as long as you please. So if you were to keep our Lord well and recollectedly, after Communion, you would long feel that devouring fire, which would inspire your heart with an inclination to good and a repugnance to evil.

When we have the good God in our heart, it ought to be very burning. The heart of the disciples of Emmaus burnt within them from merely listening to His voice.

I do not like people to begin to read directly when they come from the holy table. Oh, no!

what is the use of the words of men when God is speaking? We must do like one who is very curious, and listens at the door. We must listen to all that God says at the door of our heart.

When you have received our Lord, you feel your soul purified, because it bathes itself in the love of God.

When we go to Holy Communion, we feel something extraordinary, a comfort which pervades the whole body, and penetrates to the extremities. What is this comfort? It is our Lord, who communicates Himself to all parts of our bodies, and makes them thrill. We are obliged to say, like St. John, " It is the Lord!" Those who feel absolutely nothing are very much to be pitied.

XIII.

CATECHISM ON FREQUENT COMMUNION.

My brethren, all beings in creation require to be fed, that they may live; for this purpose God has made trees and plants grow; it is a well-served table, to which all animals come and take the food which suits each one. But the soul also must be fed. Where, then, is its food?

My brethren, the food of the soul is God. Ah! what a beautiful thought! The soul can feed on nothing but God. Only God can suffice for it; only God can fill it; only God can satiate its hunger: it absolutely requires its God! There is in all houses a place where the provisions of the family are kept; it is the storeroom. The church is the home of souls; it is the house belonging to us who are Christians. Well, in this house there is a store-room. Do you see the tabernacle? If the souls of Christians were asked, "What is that?" your souls would answer, "It is the store-room." . . .

There is nothing so great, my children, as the Eucharist! Put all the good works in the world against one good Communion; they will be like a grain of dust beside a mountain. Make a prayer when you have the good God in your heart; the good God will not be able to refuse you any thing, if you offer Him His Son, and the merits of His holy Death and passion.

My children, if we understood the value of Holy Communion, we should avoid the least faults, that we might have the happiness of making it oftener. We should keep our souls always pure in the eyes of God. My children, I suppose that you have been to confession to-day, and you will watch over yourselves; you will be happy in the thought that to-morrow you will have the joy of receiving the good God into your heart. . . . Neither can you offend the good God to-morrow; your soul will be all embalmed with the precious Blood of our Lord. . . . Oh, beautiful life!

O my children, how beautiful will a soul be in eternity that has worthily and often received the good God! The Body of our Lord will shine through our body, His adorable Blood through our blood; our soul will be united to the Soul of our Lord during all eternity. There it will enjoy pure and perfect happiness. My children, when the soul of a Christian who has received our Lord enters paradise, it augments the joy of heaven. The Angels and the Queen of Angels come to meet it, because they recognise the Son of God in that soul. Then will that soul be rewarded for the pains and sacrifices it will have endured in its life on earth.

My children, we know when a soul has worthily received the Sacrament of the Eucharist. It is so drowned in love, so penetrated and changed, that it is no longer to be recognised in its words or its actions. . . . It is humble, it is gentle, it is mortified, charitable, and modest; it is at peace with every one. It is a soul capable of the greatest sacrifices; in short, you would not know it again.

Go, then, to Communion, my children; go to Jesus with love and confidence; go and live upon Him, in order to live for Him! Do not say that you have too much to do. Has not the Divine Saviour said, "Come to me, all you that labour and are burdened, and I will refresh you"? Can you resist an invitation so full of love and tenderness? Do not say that you are not worthy of it. It is true, you are not worthy of it; but you are in need of it. If our Lord had regarded our worthiness, He would never have instituted His beautiful Sacrament of love; for no one in the world is worthy of it, neither the saints, nor the angels, nor the archangels, nor the Blessed Virgin; but He had in view our needs, and we all are in need of it. Do not say that you are sinners, that you are too miserable, and for that reason you do not dare to approach it. I would as soon hear you say that you are very ill, and that therefore you will not take any remedy, nor send for the physician.

All the prayers of the Mass are a preparation for Communion; and all the life of a Christian ought to be a preparation for that great action.

We ought to labour to deserve to receive our Lord every day. How humbled we ought to feel when we see others going to the holy table, and we remain motionless in our place! How happy is a guardian angel who leads a beautiful soul to the holy table! In the primitive Church they communicated every day. When Christians had grown cold, they substituted blessed bread for the Body of our Lord; this is both a consolation and a humiliation. It is indeed blessed bread; but it is not the Body and Blood of our Lord!

There are some who make a spiritual communion every day with blessed bread. If we are deprived of sacramental communion, let us replace it, as far as we can, by spiritual communion, which we can make every moment; for we ought to have always a burning desire to receive the good God. Communion is to the soul like blowing a fire that is beginning to go out, but that has still plenty of hot embers; we blow, and the fire burns again. After the reception of the Sacraments, when we feel ourselves slacken in the love of God, let us have recourse at once to spiritual communion. When we cannot come to church, let us turn towards the tabernacle: a wall cannot separate us from the good God; let us say five *Paters* and five *Aves* to make a spiritual communion. We can receive the good God only once a-day; a soul on fire with love supplies for this by the desire to receive Him every moment.

O man, how great thou art! fed with the Body and Blood of a God! Oh, how sweet a life is this life of union with the good God! It is heaven upon earth; there are no more troubles, no more crosses! When you have the happiness of having received the good God, you feel a joy, a sweetness in your heart for some moments. Pure souls feel it always, and in this union consists their strength and their happiness.

XIV.

CATECHISM ON SIN.

Sin is the executioner of the good God, and the assassin of the soul. It snatches us away from heaven, to precipitate us into hell. And we love it! What folly! If we thought seriously about it, we should have such a lively horror of sin that we could not commit it.

O my children, how ungrateful we are! The good God wishes to make us happy, that is very certain; He gave us His Law for no other end. The Law of God is great; it is broad. King David said that he found his delight in it, and that it was a treasure more precious to him than the greatest riches. He said also that he walked at large, because he had sought after the commandments of the Lord. The good God wishes, then, to make us happy, and we do not wish to be so. We turn away from Him, and give ourselves to the devil! We fly from our Friend, and we seek after our murderer! We commit sin; we plunge ourselves into the mire. Once sunk in this mire, we know not how to get out. If our fortune were in the case, we should soon find out how to get out of the difficulty; but because it only concerns our soul, we stay where we are.

We come to confession quite preoccupied with the shame that we shall feel. We accuse ourselves *by steam*. It is said that many confess, and few are converted. I believe it is so, my children, because few confess with tears of repentance.

See, the misfortune is that people do not reflect. If one said to those who work on Sundays, to a young person who had been dancing for two or three hours, to a man coming out of an alehouse drunk, "What have you been doing? You have been crucifying our Lord!" they would be quite astonished, because they do not think of it. My children, if we thought of it, we should be seized with horror; it would be impossible for us to do evil. For what has the good God done to us that we should grieve Him thus, and put Him to death afresh—Him, who has redeemed us from hell?

It would be well if all sinners, when they are going to their guilty pleasures, could, like St. Peter, meet our Lord on the way, who would say to them, "I am going to that place where thou art going thyself, to be there crucified afresh." Perhaps that might make them reflect.

The saints understood how great an outrage sin is against God. Some of them passed their lives in weeping for their sins. St. Peter wept all his life; he was still weeping at his death. St. Bernard used to say, "Lord! Lord! it is I who fastened Thee to the cross!"

By sin we despise the good God, we crucify the good God! What a pity it is to lose our souls, which have cost our Lord so many sufferings! What harm has our Lord done us, that we should treat Him so? If the poor lost souls could come back to the earth! if they were in our place!

Oh, how senseless we are! the good God calls us to Him, and we fly from Him! He wishes to make us happy, and we will not have His happiness. He commands us to love Him, and we give our heart to the devil. We employ in ruining ourselves the time he gives us to save our souls. We make war upon Him with the means He gave us to serve Him.

When we offend the good God, if we were to look at our crucifix, we should hear our Lord saying to us in the depths of our soul, "Wilt thou too, then, take the side of My enemies? Wilt thou crucify Me afresh?" Cast your eyes on our Lord fastened to the Cross, and say to yourself, " That is what it cost my Saviour to repair the injury my sins have done to God!" A God coming down to earth to be the victim of our sins, a God suffering, a God dying, a God enduring every torment, because He would bear the weight of our crimes! At the sight of the Cross, let us understand the malice of sin, and the hatred we ought to feel for it. Let us enter into ourselves ; let us see what we can do to make amends for our poor life.

"What a pity it is!" the good God will say to us at our death ; "why hast thou offended Me—Me, who loved thee so much?" To offend the good God, who has never done us any thing but good ; to please the devil, who can never do us any thing but evil! What folly!

Is it not real folly to choose to make ourselves worthy of hell by attaching ourselves to the devil, when we might taste the joys of heaven, even in this life, by uniting ourselves with God by love? One cannot understand this folly ; it cannot be enough lamented. Poor sinners seem as if they could not wait for the sentence which will condemn them to the society of the devils; they condemn themselves to it.

There is a sort of foretaste in this life of paradise, of hell, and of purgatory. Purgatory is in those souls that are not dead to themselves; hell is in the heart of the impious; paradise in that of the perfect, who are closely united to our Lord.

XV.

ON THE SAME SUBJECT.

He who lives in sin takes up the habits and the appearance of the beasts. The beast, which has not reason, knows nothing but its appetites. So the man who makes himself like the beasts loses his reason, and lets himself be guided by the inclinations of his body. He takes his pleasure in good eating and drinking, and in enjoying the vanities of the world, which pass away like the wind. I pity the poor wretches who run after that wind; they gain very little, they give a great deal for very little profit, —they give their eternity for the miserable smoke of the world.

My children, how sad it is! when a soul is in a state of sin, it may die in that state; and even now, whatever it can do is without merit before God. That is the reason why the devil is so pleased when a soul is in sin, and perseveres in it, because he thinks that it is working for him, and that if it were to die he would have possession of it. When we are in sin, our soul is all diseased, all rotten ; . . . it is pitiful. . . . The thought that the good God sees it ought to make it enter into itself. . . . And then, what pleasure is there in sin ? None at all. We have frightful dreams that the devil is carrying us away, that we are falling over precipices. . . . Put yourself on good terms with God; have recourse to the Sacrament of Penance; you will sleep as quietly as an angel. You will be glad to waken in the night, to pray to God; you will have nothing but thanksgivings on your lips ; you will rise towards heaven with great facility, as an eagle soars through the air.

See, my children, how sin degrades man ; of an angel created to love God it makes a demon who will curse Him for all eternity. Ah ! if Adam, our first father, had not sinned, and if we did not sin every day, how happy we should be! we should be as happy as the saints in heaven. There would be no more unhappy people on the earth. Oh, how beautiful it would be !

In fact, my children, it is sin that brings upon us all calamities, all scourges, war, famine,

pestilence, earthquakes, fires, frost, hail, storms,
—all that afflicts us, all that makes us miserable.

See, my children, a person who is in a state of sin is always sad. Whatever he does, he is weary and disgusted with every thing; while he who is at peace with God is always happy, always joyous. . . . Oh, beautiful life! Oh, beautiful death!

My children, we are afraid of death; I can well believe it. It is sin that makes us afraid of death; it is sin that renders death frightful, formidable; it is sin that terrifies the wicked at the hour of the fearful passage. Alas! O God! there is reason enough to be terrified, to think that one is accursed—accursed of God! It makes one tremble. Accursed of God! and why? for what do men expose themselves to be accursed of God? For a blasphemy, for a bad thought, for a bottle of wine, for two minutes of pleasure! For two minutes of pleasure to lose God, one's soul, heaven, for ever! We shall see going up to heaven, in body and soul, that father, that mother, that sister, that neighbour, who were here with us, with whom we have lived, but whom we have not imitated; while we shall go down body and soul to burn in hell. The devils will rush to overwhelm us. All the devils whose advice we followed will come to torment us.

My children, if you saw a man prepare a great pile of wood, heaping up fagots one upon another, and when you asked him what he was doing, he were to answer you, " I am preparing the fire that is to burn me," what would you think ? And if you saw this same man set fire to the pile, and when it was lighted throw himself upon it, what would you say ? This is what we do when we commit sin. It is not God who casts us into hell; we cast ourselves into it by our sins. The lost soul will say, "I have lost God, my soul, and heaven; it is through my fault, through my fault, through my most grievous fault!" He will raise himself out of the fire only to fall back into it. He will always feel the desire of rising because he was created for God, the greatest, the highest of beings, the Most High, . . . as a bird shut up in a room flies to the ceiling, and falls down again; the justice of God is the ceiling which keeps down the lost.

There is no need to prove the existence of hell. Our Lord Himself speaks of it when He relates the history of the wicked rich man who cried out, "Lazarus! Lazarus!" We know very well that there is a hell, but we live as if there were not; we sell our souls for a few pieces of money. We put off our conversion till the hour of death; but who can assure us that we shall have time or strength at that formidable moment, which has been feared by all the saints—when hell will gather itself up for a last assault upon us, seeing that it is the decisive moment? There are many people who lose the faith, and never see hell till they enter it. The Sacraments are administered to them; but ask them if they have committed such a sin, and they will answer you, "Oh! settle that as you please." . . .

Some people offend the good God every moment; their heart is an ant-hill of sins: it is like a spoilt piece of meat, half-eaten by worms. . . .

No, indeed; if sinners were to think of eternity—of that terrible FOR EVER!—they would be converted instantly. Cain has been in hell nearly six thousand years, and he is only just entering it.

XVI.

CATECHISM ON PRIDE.

PRIDE is that accursed sin which drove the angels out of paradise, and hurled them into hell. This sin began with the world.

See, my children, we sin by pride in many

ways. A person may be proud in his clothes, in his language, in his gestures, even in his manner of walking. Some persons, when they are in the streets, walk along proudly, and seem to say to the people they meet, "Look how tall, how upright I am, how well I walk!" . . . Others, when they have done any good action, are never tired of talking of it ; and if they fail in any thing, they are miserable, because they think people will have a bad opinion of them; . . . others are sorry to be seen with the poor, if they meet with any body of consequence; they are always seeking the company of the rich; . . . if, by chance, they are noticed by the great people of the world, they boast and are vain of it. Others take pride in speaking. If they go to see rich people, they consider what they are going to say, they study fine language; and if they make a mistake of a word, they are very much vexed, because they are afraid of being laughed at. But, my children, with a humble person it is not so . . . whether he is laughed at or esteemed, or praised or blamed, whether he is honoured or despised, whether people pay attention to him or pass him by, it is all the same to him.

My children, there are again people who give great alms, that they may be well thought of—that will not do! These people will reap no fruit from their good works. On the contrary, their alms will turn into sins.

We put pride into every thing, like salt. We like to see that our good works are known. If our virtues are seen, we are pleased; if our faults are perceived, we are sad. I remark that in a great many people; if one says any thing to them, it disturbs them, it annoys them. The saints were not like that—they were vexed if their virtues were known, and pleased that their imperfections should be seen.

A proud person thinks every thing he does is well done; he wants to domineer over all those who have to do with him; he is always right, he always thinks his own opinion better than that of others; .... that will not do! A humble and well-taught person, if he is asked his opinion, gives it at once, and then lets others speak. Whether they are right or whether they are wrong, he says nothing more.

When St. Aloysius Gonzaga was a student, he never sought to excuse himself when he was reproached with any thing; he said what he thought, and troubled himself no further about what others might think: if he was wrong, he was wrong; if he was right, he said to himself, "I have certainly been wrong some other time."

My children, the saints were so completely

dead to themselves, that they cared very little whether others agreed with them. People in the world say, "Oh, the saints were simpletons!" Yes, they were simpletons in worldly things; but in the things of God they were very wise. They understood nothing about worldly matters, to be sure, because they thought them of so little importance that they paid no attention to them.

XVII.

CATECHISM ON IMPURITY.

THAT we may understand how horrible and detestable is this sin, which the demons make us commit, but which they do not commit themselves, we must consider what a Christian is. . . . A Christian, created in the image of God, redeemed by the Blood of a God! a Christian, the child of God, the brother of a God, the heir of a God! a Christian, the object of the complacency of the Three Divine Persons! a Christian, whose body is the temple of the Holy Ghost; that is what sin dishonours.

We are created to reign one day in heaven, and if we have the misfortune to commit this sin, we become the den of the devils. Our Lord said that nothing impure should enter into His kingdom. Indeed, how could a soul that has rolled itself in this filth go to appear before so pure and so holy a God?

We are all like little mirrors, in which God contemplates Himself. How can you expect that God should recognise His likeness in an impure soul?

There are some souls so dead, so *rotten*, that they lie in their defilement without perceiving it, and can no longer clear themselves from it: every thing leads them to evil, every thing reminds them of evil, even the most holy things; they always have these abominations before their eyes; like the unclean animal that is accustomed to live in filth, that is happy in it, that rolls itself and goes to sleep in it, that grunts in the mud; these persons are an object of horror in the eyes of God and of the holy angels.

See, my children: our Lord was crowned with thorns to expiate our sins of pride; but for this accursed sin, He was scourged and torn to pieces, since He said Himself that after His flagellation all His bones might be counted.

O my children, if there were not some pure souls here and there, to make amends to the good God, and disarm His justice, you would see how we should be punished! . . . For now, this crime is so common in the world, that it is enough to make one tremble. One may say, my children, that hell vomits forth its abominations upon the earth, as the chimneys of the steam-engine vomit forth smoke.

The devil does all he can to defile our soul, and yet our soul is every thing; . . . our body is only a heap of corruption: go to the cemetery to see what you love, when you love your body.

As I have often told you, there is nothing so vile as the impure soul. There was once a saint who had asked the good God to show him one; and he saw that poor soul like a dead beast that has been dragged through the streets in the hot sun for a week.

By only looking at a person, we know if he is pure. His eyes have an air of candour and modesty which leads you to the good God. Some people, on the contrary, look quite inflamed with passion. . . . Satan places himself in their eyes to make others fall and to lead them to evil.

Those who have lost their purity are like a piece of cloth stained with oil; you may wash it and dry it, and the stain always appears again: so it requires a miracle to cleanse the impure soul.

XVIII.

CATECHISM ON CONFESSION.

My children, as soon as ever you have a little spot upon your soul, you must do like a person who has a fine globe of glass, which he keeps very carefully. If this globe has a little dust on it, he wipes it with a sponge the moment he perceives it, and there is the globe clear and brilliant. In the same way, as soon as you perceive a little stain on your soul, take some holy water with respect, do one of those good works to which the remission of venial sins is attached—an alms, a genuflexion to the Blessed Sacrament, hearing a Mass. . . .

My children, it is like a person who has a slight illness; he need not go and see a doctor, he may cure himself without. If he has a headache, he need only go to bed; if he is hungry, he has only to eat. But if it is a serious illness, if it is a dangerous wound, he must have the doctor; after the doctor come the remedies. In the same way, when we have fallen into any grievous sin, we must have recourse to the doctor, that is the priest; and to the remedy, that is confession.

My children, we cannot comprehend the goodness of God towards us in instituting this great

Sacrament of Penance. If we had had a favour to ask of our Lord, we should never have thought of asking Him that. But He foresaw our frailty and our inconstancy in well-doing, and His love induced Him to do what we should not have dared to ask.

If one said to those poor lost souls that have been so long in hell, "We are going to place a priest at the gate of hell : all those who wish to confess have only to go out," do you think, my children, that a single one would remain? The most guilty would not be afraid of telling their sins, nor even of telling them before all the world. Oh, how soon hell would be a desert, and how heaven would be peopled! Well, we have the time and the means which those poor lost souls have not. And I am quite sure that these wretched ones say in hell, "O accursed priest, if I had never known you, I should not be so guilty!"

It is a beautiful thought, my children, that we have a Sacrament which heals the wounds of our soul! But we must receive it with good dispositions. Otherwise we make new wounds upon the old ones. What would you say of a man covered with wounds, who is advised to go to the hospital to show himself to the surgeon? The surgeon cures him by giving him remedies. But, behold! this man takes his knife, gives himself great blows with it, and makes himself worse than he was before. Well, that is what you often do after leaving the confessional.

My children, some people make bad confessions without taking any notice of it. These persons say, "I do not know what is the matter with me." . . . They are tormented, and they do not know why. They have not that agility which makes one go straight to the good God; they have something heavy and weary about them which fatigues them. My children, that is because of sins that remain, often even venial sins, for which one has some affection. There are some people who, indeed, tell every thing, but they have no repentance; and they go at once to Holy Communion. Thus the Blood of our Lord is profaned! They go to the Holy Table with a sort of weariness. They say, "Yet, I accused myself of all my sins. . . . I do not know what is the matter with me." There is an unworthy communion, and they were hardly aware of it!

My children, some people again profane the Sacraments in another manner. They have concealed mortal sins for ten years, for twenty years. They are always uneasy; their sin is always present to their mind; they are always thinking of confessing it, and always putting it off; it is a hell. When these people feel this, they will ask to make a general confession, and they will tell their sins as if they had just committed them; they will not confess that they have hidden them during ten years—twenty years. That is a bad confession!... They ought to say, besides, that they had given up the practice of their religion, that they no longer felt the pleasure they had formerly in serving the good God.

My children, we run the risk again of profaning the Sacrament, if we seize the moment when there is a noise round the confessional to tell the sins quickly which give us most pain. We quiet ourselves by saying, "I accused myself properly; so much the worse if the confessor did not hear." So much the worse for you who acted cunningly!... At other times we speak quickly, profiting by the moment when the priest is not very attentive to get over the great sins.

Take a house which has been for a long time very dirty and neglected—it is in vain to sweep it out, there will always be a nasty smell. It is the same with our soul after confession; it requires tears to purify it.

My children, we must ask earnestly for repentance. After confession, we must plant a thorn in our heart, and never lose sight of our sins. We must do as the angel did to St. Francis of Assisi; he fixed in him five darts, which never came out again.

XIX.

CATECHISM ON THE CARDINAL VIRTUES.

* * * * * *

PRUDENCE shows us what is most pleasing to God, and most useful to the salvation of our soul. We must always choose the most perfect. Two good works present themselves to be done, one in favour of a person we love, the other in favour of a person who has done us some harm; well, we must give the preference to the latter.

There is no merit in doing good, when a natural feeling leads us to do it. A lady wishing to have a widow to live with her to take care of, asked St. Athanasius to find her one among his poor. Afterwards meeting the Bishop, she reproached him that he had treated her ill, because this person was too good, and gave her nothing to do by which she could gain heaven; and she begged him to give her another. The saint chose the worst he could find; of a cross, grumbling temper, never satisfied with what was done for her. This is the way we must act, for there is no great merit in doing good to one who values it, who thanks us and is grateful.

There are some persons who think they are never treated well enough; they seem as if they had a right to every thing. They are never pleased with what is done for them; they repay every body with ingratitude. . . . Well! those are the people to whom we should do good by preference. We must be prudent in all our actions, and seek not our own taste, but what is most pleasing to the good God. Suppose you have a franc that you intend to give for a Mass; you see a poor family in distress, in want of bread: it is better to give your money to these wretched people, because the Holy Sacrifice will still be offered; the priest will not fail to say holy Mass; while these poor people may die of hunger. . . . You would wish to pray to the good God, to pass your whole day in the church; but you think it would be very useful to work for some poor people that you know, who are in great need; that is much more pleasing to God than your day passed before the holy tabernacle.

Temperance is another cardinal virtue; we can be temperate in the use of our imagination, by not letting it gallop as fast as it would wish; we can be temperate with our eyes, temperate with our mouth—some people constantly have something sweet and pleasant in their mouth; we can be temperate with our ears, not allowing them to listen to useless songs and conversation; temperate in smelling —some people perfume themselves to such a degree as to make those about them sick; temperate with the hands—some people are always washing them when it is hot, and handling things that are soft to the touch. . . . In short, we can practise temperance with our whole body, this poor machine, by not letting it run away like a horse without bit or bridle, but checking it and keeping it down. Some people lie buried there, in their beds; . . . they are glad not to sleep, that they may the better feel how comfortable they are. The saints were not like that. I do not know how we are ever to get where they are. . . . Well! if we are saved, we shall stay infinitely long in purgatory, while they will fly straight to heaven to see the good God.

That great saint, St. Charles Borromeo, had in his apartment a fine cardinal's bed, which every body saw; but, besides that, there was one which nobody could see, made of bundles of wood; and that was the one he made use of. He never warmed himself; when people came to see him, they remarked that he placed himself so as not to feel the fire. That is what the saints were like. They lived for heaven, and not for earth: they were all heavenly; and as for us, we are all earthly.

Oh, how I like those little mortifications that are seen by nobody, such as rising a quarter of an hour sooner, rising for a little while in the night to pray! but some people think of nothing but sleeping.

There was once a solitary who had built himself a royal palace in the trunk of an oak-tree; he had placed thorns inside of it, and he had fastened three stones over his head, so that when he raised himself or turned over he might feel the stones or the thorns. And we, we think of nothing but finding good beds, that we may sleep at our ease.

We may refrain from warming ourselves; if we are sitting uncomfortably, we need not try to place ourselves better; if we are walking in our garden, we may deprive ourselves of some fruit that we should like; in preparing the food, we need not eat the little bits that offer themselves; we may deprive ourselves of seeing something pretty, which attracts our eyes, especially in the streets of great towns. There is a gentleman who sometimes comes here. He wears two pairs of spectacles, that he may see nothing. . . . But some heads are always in motion, some eyes are always looking about. . . . When we are going along the streets, let us fix our eyes on our Lord carrying His cross before us; on the Blessed Virgin, who is looking at us; on our guardian angel, who is by our side. How beautiful is this interior life! It unites us with the good God. . . . Therefore, when the devil sees a soul that is seeking to attain to it, he tries to turn him aside from it by filling his imagination with a thousand fancies. A good Christian does not listen to that; he goes always forward in perfection, like a fish plunging into the depths of the sea. . . . As for us, alas! we drag ourselves along like a leech in the mud.

There were two saints in the desert, who had sewed thorns into all their clothes; and we seek for nothing but comfort! Yet we wish to go to heaven, but with all our luxuries, without having any annoyance; that is not the way the saints acted. They sought every way of mortifying themselves, and in the midst of all their privations they tasted infinite sweetness. How happy are those who love the good God! They do not lose a single opportunity of doing good; misers employ all the means in their power to increase their treasure; they do the same for the riches of heaven—they are always heaping up. . . . We shall be surprised at the Day of Judgment to see souls so rich!

XX.

CATECHISM ON HOPE.

My children, we are going to speak of hope: this is what makes the happiness of man on earth. Some people in this world hope too much, and others do not hope enough. Some say, "I am going to commit this sin again. It will not cost me more to confess four than three." It is like a child saying to his father, "I am going to give you four blows; it will cost me no more than to give you one: I shall only have to ask your pardon."

That is the way men behave towards the good God. They say, "This year I shall amuse myself again; I shall go to dances and to the alehouse, and next year I will be converted. The good God will be sure to receive me, when I choose to return to Him. He is not so cruel as the priests tell us." . . . No; the good God is not cruel, but He is just. Do you think he will adapt Himself in every thing to your will? Do you think that He will embrace you, after you have despised Him all your life? Oh, no, indeed! There is a certain measure of grace and of sin after which God withdraws Himself. What would you say of a father who should treat a good child, and one not so good, in the same manner? You would say, this father is not just. Well! God would not be just if He made no difference between those who serve Him and those who offend Him.

My children, there is so little faith now in the world, that people either hope too much, or they despair. Some say, "I have done too much evil; the good God cannot pardon me." My children, this is a great blasphemy; it is putting a limit to the mercy of God, which has no limit—it is infinite. You may have done evil enough to lose the souls of a whole parish, and if you confess, if you are sorry for having done this evil, and resolve not to do it again, the good God will have pardoned you.

A priest was once preaching on hope, and on the mercy of the good God. He reassured others, but he himself despaired. After the sermon, a young man presented himself, saying, "Father, I am come to confess to you." The priest answered, "I am willing to hear your confession." The other recounted his sins; after which he added, "Father, I have done much evil; I am lost!" . . . "What do you say, my friend? we must never despair." . . . The young man rose, saying, "Father, you wish me not to despair, and what do you do?" This was a ray of light; the priest, all astonishment, drove away that thought of despair, became a religious and a great saint. . . . The good God had sent him an angel under the form of a young man, to show him that we must never despair.

The good God is as prompt to grant us pardon when we ask it of Him, as a mother is to snatch her child out of the fire.

XXI.

CATECHISM ON SUFFERING.

WHETHER we will or no, we must suffer. There are some who suffer like the good thief, and others like the bad thief. They both suffered equally. But one knew how to make his sufferings meritorious; he accepted them in the spirit of reparation, and turning towards Jesus crucified, he received from His mouth these beautiful words: "This day thou shalt be with Me in Paradise." The other, on the contrary, cried out, uttered imprecations and blasphemies, and expired in the most frightful despair.

There are two ways of suffering—to suffer with love, and to suffer without love. The saints suffered every thing with joy, patience, and perseverance, because they loved. As for us, we suffer with anger, vexation, and weariness, because we do not love. If we loved God, we should love crosses, we should wish for them, we should take pleasure in them. . . . We should be happy to be able to suffer for the love of Him who lovingly suffered for us. Of what do we complain? Alas! the poor infidels, who have not the happiness of knowing God and His infinite loveliness, have the same crosses that we have; but they have not the same consolations.

You say it is hard? No, it is easy, it is consoling, it is sweet; it is happiness. Only we must love while we suffer, and suffer while we love.

On the Way of the Cross, you see, my children, only the first step is painful. Our greatest cross is the fear of crosses. . . . We have not the courage to carry our cross, and we are very much mistaken; for, whatever we do, the cross holds us tight—we cannot escape from it. What, then, have we to lose? Why not love our crosses, and make use of them to take us to heaven? . . . But, on the contrary, most men turn their backs upon crosses, and fly before them. The more they run, the more the cross pursues them, the more it strikes and crushes them with burdens. . . . If you were wise, you would go to meet it like St. Andrew, who said, when he saw the cross prepared for him and raised up into the air, " Hail, O good cross ! O admirable cross ! O desirable cross! receive me into thy arms, withdraw me from among men, and restore me to my Master, who redeemed me through thee."

Listen attentively to this, my children: He who goes to meet the cross, goes in the opposite direction to crosses; he meets them, perhaps, but he is pleased to meet them; he loves them; he carries them courageously. They unite him to our Lord ; they purify him; they detach him from this world; they remove all obstacles from his heart ; they help him to pass through life, as a bridge helps us to pass over water. . . . Look at the saints; when they were not persecuted, they persecuted themselves. . . . A good religious complained one day to our Lord that he was persecuted. He said, " O Lord, what have I done to be treated thus?" Our Lord answered him, " And I, what had I done when I was led to Calvary ?" . . . Then the religious understood ; he wept, he asked pardon, and dared not complain any more.

Worldly people are miserable when they have crosses, and good Christians are miserable when they have none. The Christian lives in the midst of crosses, as the fish lives in the sea.

Look at St. Catherine; she has two crowns, that of purity and that of martyrdom: how happy she is, that dear little saint, to have chosen to suffer rather than to consent to sin! There was once a religious who loved suffering so much, that he had fastened the rope from a well round his body; this cord had rubbed off the skin, and had by degrees buried itself in the flesh, out of which worms came. The religious asked that he should be sent out of the community. He went away happy and pleased, to hide himself in a rocky cavern. But the same night the superior heard our Lord saying to him: "Thou hast lost the treasure of thy house." Then they went to fetch back this good saint, and they wanted to see from whence these worms came. The superior had the cords taken off, which was done by turning back the flesh. At last he got well.

Very near this, in a neighbouring parish, there was a little boy in bed covered with sores, very ill, and very miserable; I said to him, "My poor little child, you are suffering very much!" He answered me, "No, sir; to-day I do not feel the pain I had yesterday, and to-morrow I shall not suffer from the pain I have now." "You would like to get well?" "No; I was naughty before I was ill, and I might be so again. I am very well as I am." . . . . It was vinegar indeed, but there was more oil. . . . We do not understand that, because we are too earthly. Children in whom the Holy Ghost dwells put us to shame.

If the good God sends us crosses, we resist, we complain, we murmur; we are so averse to whatever contradicts us, that we want to be always in a box of cotton: but we ought to be put into a box of thorns. It is by the Cross that we go to heaven. Illnesses, temptations, troubles, are so many crosses which take us to heaven. All this will soon be over. . . . Look at the saints, who have arrived there before us. . . . The good God does not require of us the martyrdom of the body; He requires only the martyrdom of the heart, and of the will. . . . Our Lord is our model; let us take up our cross, and follow Him. Let us do like the soldiers of Napoleon. They had to cross a bridge under the fire of grape-shot; no one dared to pass it. Napoleon took the colours, marched over first, and they all followed. Let us do the same; let us follow our Lord, who has gone before us.

A soldier was telling me one day, that during a battle he had marched for half an hour over dead bodies; there was hardly space to tread upon; the ground was all dyed with blood. Thus on the road of life we must walk over crosses and troubles to reach our true country.

The cross is the ladder to heaven. . . . How consoling it is to suffer under the eyes of God, and to be able to say in the evening, at our examination of conscience: "Come, my soul! thou hast had to-day two or three hours of resemblance to Jesus Christ. Thou hast been scourged, crowned with thorns, crucified with Him!" . . . Oh, what a treasure for the hour of death! . . . How sweet it is to die, when we have lived on the cross!

We ought to run after crosses as the miser runs after money. . . Nothing but crosses will reassure us at the Day of Judgment. When that day shall come, we shall be happy in our misfortunes, proud of our humiliations, and rich in our sacrifices!

If some one said to you, "I should like to become rich; what must I do?" you would answer him, "You must labour." Well, in order to get to heaven, we must suffer. Our Lord shows us the way in the person of Simon the Cyrenian; He calls His friends to carry His cross after Him.

The good God wishes us never to lose sight of the Cross, therefore it is placed every where; by the roadside, on the heights, in the public squares—in order that at the sight of it we may say, "See how God has loved us!"

The Cross embraces the world; it is planted at the four corners of the world; there is a share of it for all.

Crosses are on the road to heaven like a fine bridge of stone over a river, by which to pass it. Christians who do not suffer, pass this river by a frail bridge, a bridge of wire, always ready to give way under their feet.

He who does not love the Cross may indeed be saved, but with great difficulty: he will be a little star in the firmament. He who shall have suffered and fought for his God will shine like a beautiful sun.

Crosses, transformed by the flames of love, are like a bundle of thorns thrown into the fire, and reduced by the fire to ashes. The thorns are hard, but the ashes are soft.

Oh, how much sweetness do souls experience that are all for God in suffering! It is like a mixture into which one puts a deal of oil: the vinegar remains vinegar; but the oil corrects its bitterness, and it can scarcely be perceived.

If you put fine grapes into the wine-press, there will come out a delicious juice: our soul, in the wine-press of the Cross, gives out a juice that nourishes and strengthens it. When we have no crosses, we are arid: if we bear them with resignation, we feel a joy, a happiness, a sweetness! . . . it is the beginning of heaven. The good God, the Blessed Virgin, the angels, and the saints, surround us; they are by our side, and see us. The passage to the other life, of the good Christian tried by affliction, is like that of a person being carried on a bed of roses.

Thorns give out perfume, and the Cross breathes forth sweetness. But we must squeeze the thorns in our hands, and press the Cross to our heart, that they may give out the juice they contain.

The Cross gave peace to the world; and it must bring peace to our hearts. All our miseries come from our not loving it. The fear of crosses increases them. A cross carried simply, and without those returns of self-love which exaggerate troubles, is no longer a cross. Peaceable suffering is no longer suffering. We complain of suffering! we should have much more reason to complain of not suffering, since nothing makes us more like our Lord than carrying His cross. Oh, what a beautiful union of the soul with our Lord Jesus Christ by the love and the virtue of His Cross! I do not understand how a Christian can dislike the Cross, and fly from it! does he not at the same time fly from Him who has deigned to be fastened to it, and to die for us?

Contradictions bring us to the foot of the Cross, and the Cross to the gate of heaven. That we may get there, we must be trodden upon, we must be set at naught, despised, crushed. . . . There are no happy people in this world but those who enjoy calmness of mind in the midst of the troubles of life: they taste the joy of the children of God. . . . All pains are sweet when we suffer in union with our Lord. . . .

To suffer! what does it signify? It is only a moment. If we could go and pass a week in heaven, we should understand the value of this moment of suffering. We should find no cross heavy enough, no trial bitter enough. . . . The Cross is the gift that God makes to His friends.

How beautiful it is to offer ourselves every morning in sacrifice to the good God, and to accept every thing in expiation of our sins! . . . We must ask for the love of crosses; then they become sweet. I tried it for four or five years. I was well calumniated, well contradicted, well knocked about. Oh, I had crosses indeed! I had almost more than I could carry!

Then I took to asking for love of crosses, and I was happy. I said to myself, Truly there is no happiness but in this! . . . We must never think from whence crosses come: they come from God. It is always God who gives us this way of proving our love to Him.

PART II.

THE CURÉ OF ARS IN HIS HOMILIES.

THOSE who have heard M. Vianney only in his catechisms do but half know him. They know the infused light, the supernatural grace, the solidity, transparency, depth, and originality of his discourses; but they do not know their life, their fire, and their unction. It was in his Sunday homilies that the missionary, the apostolic man, the oracle, the inspired prophet, the saint consumed by zeal for the salvation of souls, showed himself under a rare and inimitable aspect, in all the power and fascination of his individual character. They were distinguished by a mixture of loftiness and tenderness, of lively and ardent faith, of impetuous zeal, which gave the preacher such power and unction as to produce the strongest emotions in his hearers. Hence those marvellous effects that have been so often observed at Ars; that change of heart, that submission of the will, those tears, that deep emotion, which began before the pulpit, and was completed in the secret intercourse of the confessional.

The eloquence of his voice was enhanced by

the eloquence of his personal appearance. His broad forehead, with its aureola of white hair, his bold profile, the beatific expression of the holy man's countenance, and, above all, the ever-varying fire of his glance, gave him a sort of supernatural fascination, before which we have often seen the proudest spirits bend, and scepticism declare itself conquered.

The style which he adopted in his homilies interested, captivated, and instructed his hearers, whoever they might be. Yet we must own that the eloquence of the holy curé was destitute of all those extraneous ornaments which usually contribute so much to the success of a preacher. And this is another proof of the supernatural power and divine charms of the Gospel, which, when preached in all its simplicity, triumphs no less over the poverty of him who announces it, than over the various and often exaggerated requirements of those who listen to it.

The love of our Lord is the principle of all virtues. Like material fire, this heavenly fire warms and purifies the soul. Now, the surest way of kindling this fire in the heart of the faithful is to explain to them the Gospel—that book of love—in every line of which the Saviour shows Himself in His gentleness, His patience, His humility; always the Consoler and the Friend of man, speaking to him only of love, and persuading him to devote himself entirely to Him, by returning Him love for love.

We give here but incomplete extracts, which have at least the merit of fidelity; they reproduce the thoughts, and sometimes the expression and figure of them, and they will suffice to give an idea of this style of preaching.

On the Feast of the Presentation, M. Vianney said :

"Have you meditated on the love which consumed the heart of the old man Simeon during his ecstasy? for surely he was in ecstasy when he held the Infant Jesus in his arms! He had asked the good God to let him see the Saviour of Israel, and God had promised that he should. He passed fifty years in this expectation, longing for this moment with all his heart, consumed by desire. When Mary and Joseph entered the Temple, God said to him, 'Here He is!' . . . Then, taking in his arms and pressing to his heart the Infant Jesus, who was burning and consuming that heart, the good old man cried, 'Now, O Lord, let me die!' . . . Then he gave Jesus back to His Mother; he could keep Him but for a moment. But we, my brethren, are we not much happier than Simeon? We can keep Him always with us, if we will. . . . . He comes not only into our arms, but into our hearts."

"O man, how happy thou art, but how little thou knowest thy happiness! If thou didst comprehend it, thou couldst not live. . . . Oh! no; certainly thou couldst not live!" (Here tears choked the voice of the holy curé.) "Thou wouldst die of love. . . . This God gives Himself to thee. . . . Thou canst carry Him away, if thou wilt—where thou wilt. . . . He is now one with thee! . . ."

The rest of the sermon was nothing but a series of exclamations, interrupted by tears and sobs. It often happened that the holy man was obliged to stop, overcome by his emotion. Sometimes his discourse was nothing but a cry, a sublime cry, of love, of joy, or of grief. We remember that, when he was explaining the Gospel of the Second Sunday in Lent, the ecstasy of the Apostles on Mount Thabor brought to his mind the happiness of the soul that is called to enjoy the clear vision of the Sacred Humanity of our Lord in heaven; and he exclaimed, transported out of himself, "We shall see Him! we shall see Him! . . . O my brethren! have you ever thought of this? We shall see God! we shall see Him, in good earnest! we shall see Him as He is, . . . face to face!" And for a quarter of an hour he ceased not to weep, and to repeat, "We shall see Him! we shall see Him!"

Another time, he had taken for the subject of his instruction the Last Judgment; and suddenly stopping at the words of the terrible sentence, "Depart from me, you cursed!" he burst out into tears, sighs, and sobs, and could only repeat, "Cursed of God! Oh, what a horrible misfortune! Do you understand, my children? cursed of God, who can only bless! cursed of God, who is all love! cursed of God, who is goodness itself! cursed of God!"

The audience was overwhelmed.

His discourses were sometimes coloured by contemporary events, and reflected by turns the joy and the sadness of his soul.

He said, in 1849:

"It seems that in the absence of His Vicar, our Lord comes Himself upon the earth; He reassumes His Humanity, to show Himself to men. For you have heard of the new miracle which has lately taken place at Rome. They had exposed the veil with which St. Veronica wiped the holy Face of our Lord, but which was almost effaced by time. While the Cardinals were kneeling before this divine Image, all the holy Face was seen to reappear, sad, and shedding tears. There are some who will not believe it; can a blind man distinguish colours? By this apparition and these tears, our Lord said to the Cardinals, 'Where is My

Son, your Father ? He has been driven away; where is He ?' As Mary said to St. Peter after the death of Jesus, ' Where is your Father and my Son ? I see Him no longer.' Our Lord wept for His Vicar, like a father who has lost his son, like a husband who has lost his spouse. He worked this miracle on behalf of the Pope. How holy he must be ! Therefore, how pleasing to God must be the alms of those who give to the Pope ! You will always have the poor among you, but you will not always have the opportunity of giving to the Holy Father. You will have a share in his holy prayers. Our Lord has always shown deference to His Vicar; he is the keeper of all His treasures. So we can do nothing more pleasing to God than to pray for him till he has returned to his States. This is what Jesus asks of us by His tears."

In 1830, having learnt that crosses had been thrown down in some parts of France, " They will do it in vain !" cried he, in the middle of his catechism, with an energy and indignation which made a strong impression on his hearers ; " they will do it in vain ! The Cross is stronger than they ; they will not always overthrow it. When our Lord shall appear on the clouds of heaven, they will not snatch it out of His hands !"

Three years after, God took His reprisals.

The cholera had visited Marseilles and Paris, and threatened Lyons. The holy Curé began his instruction with these serious words: "My brethren, God is going to sweep out the world!" This simple sentence, and the tone of voice in which it was spoken, made such an impression upon an artist who heard it, that it was the beginning of his conversion.

I.

HOMILY ON THE PARABLE OF THE COCKLE.

You see, my brethren, in the Gospel of to-day, that the master of the field having sown his seed on good soil, the enemy came while he was asleep, and sowed cockle among it. This means that God created man good and perfect, but that the enemy came and sowed sin. . . . There is the fall of Adam; a terrible fall, which gave sin the entrance into the heart of man. . . There is the mixture of the good and the wicked: we see sin in the midst of virtues. . . .

The cockle must be pulled up, do you say? No, answers the Lord, for fear that in pulling up the cockle you should root up the good corn. Wait till the harvest. . . . The heart of man must thus remain till the end a mixture of good and evil, of vice and virtue, of light and darkness, of good corn and cockle. . . . The good God has not willed to destroy this mixture, and to make for us a new nature, in which there should be nothing but good corn. He wills that we should fight, that we should labour, to prevent the cockle from overpowering every thing.

The devil is very anxious to sow temptations under our feet; but with grace we can defeat him, we can choke the cockle. . . . The cockle consists chiefly in impurity and pride. Without impurity and pride, says St. Augustine, there would not be much merit in resisting temptation.

Three things are absolutely necessary against temptation: prayer to enlighten us, the Sacraments to fortify us, and vigilance to preserve us. Happy are the souls that are tempted! When the devil foresees that a soul is tending towards union with God, his rage is redoubled. . . . Oh, happy union! . . .

[The rest of the homily was lost in cries of admiration of the sweetness of the interior life, and of union with God.]

II.

HOMILY ON THE PARABLE OF THE LABOURERS.

It is said in the Gospel of to-day, my brethren, that the householder went out early in the morning to hire labourers to work in his vineyard. . . . Then there was no one yet in this vineyard? Yes, my brethren, there was the most holy Virgin Mary, who was born in that vineyard. . . . What is that vineyard? It is grace; and the Blessed Virgin was born in it, since she was conceived without sin. . . .

As for us, we have been called into it. The Lord of the vineyard sought for us, but the Blessed Virgin was always there. . . . Oh, beautiful labourer! The good God could have created a more beautiful world than that which exists, but He could not have given being to a creature more perfect than Mary. . . . She is the tower built in the midst of the vineyard of the Lord. . . .

Here, my children, is a feeble comparison. You know those eggs that are in the sea, from which come little fish, which dart so swiftly through the waters. . . . In the same way the Blessed Virgin, as soon as she is created, has the fulness of life, and swims in the great ocean of grace. . . .

Besides the Blessed Virgin, there was one

who was for a moment out of the vineyard, but who was not long in entering it; that was St. John Baptist. All others came after St. John Baptist, and the Lord of the vineyard had to go out to seek them.

Who are the labourers of the first hour? St. Aloysius Gonzaga, St. Stanislas Kostka, St. Colette; . . . all those who entered into the vineyard by holy Baptism, and who never went out of it, since they preserved their innocence. . . . Happy souls who can say to God, "O Lord, I have always belonged to Thee!" Oh, how beautiful, how grand it is to give one's youth to God! What a source of joy and happiness!

Then come those who give themselves to God in the vigour of their life. They may still be sincerely converted, and remain good and faithful labourers in the vineyard of the Lord. . . . But those poor hardened sinners, who pass their lives far from God, who come to work in His vineyard when they are unable to do any thing else, who wait to give up sin till sin gives them up, . . . oh, they are very much to be pitied! When a person has revelled for years and years in evil, when he has wallowed at his ease in the mire of sin, it requires a miracle to make him leave it. My brethren, let us ask for this miracle for them. . . .

[We seem to find here, in a simple form, adapted to a country audience, the method of the ancient Fathers; their broad and luminous manner of interpreting and developing the sense of the Gospel—not stopping at the letter of it, but penetrating into the mysteries it contains, revealing its treasures of wisdom and of love, showing the harmony of the two Testaments, the accomplishment of prophecy, the relations of the past and the future, of doctrines and commandments.

Every one will observe the beauty of the comparison of the little fishes just hatched swimming in the wide seas, with the Blessed Virgin plunged from her birth in the ocean of divine grace.]

III.

HOMILY ON THE GOSPEL FOR THE FIRST SUNDAY IN LENT.

OUR Divine Lord, having been our model in every thing, would be our model in temptation also. For this end He allowed Himself to be led into the desert.

The good soldier has no fear of the battle, and so a good Christian ought to have no fear of temptation. All soldiers are good in garrison: on the field of battle we see the difference between the brave and the cowardly.

The greatest of all temptations is to have none. We may almost say that we are happy in having temptations; it is the moment of the spiritual harvest, when we lay up stores for heaven. It is like the time of harvest, when we rise very early, and take a great deal of trouble; but we do not complain, because we gather in a great deal.

The devil tempts only those souls that wish to abandon sin and those that are in a state of grace. The others belong to him: he has no need to tempt them.

A saint, passing one day before a convent, saw a quantity of devils tormenting the religious, without being able to succeed in seducing them. He passed afterwards by a town, and saw a single one sitting down with his arms across, and guiding the whole population. Then the saint asked him how he came to be alone in a great town, while there were so many tormenting a handful of religious. The devil answered him that he was quite enough for the town, because he tempted those who were already inclined to hatred, impurity, drunkenness, and it was done in a moment; while with the religious it was more difficult. The army of devils occupied in tempting them lost their time and their trouble; they could gain no ground. So they waited till others should come, who might grow weary of the austerity of the rule.

In a monastery, during the Holy Sacrifice, one of the brothers saw devils prowling round those good religious. He saw one in particular stamping on the head of a monk, and another advancing and receding by turns. After Mass, this brother asked the two religious what had occupied their minds during Office. The first said he had thought of a floor he wanted to have made in the convent; and the second said that the devil had come to attack him, but he had always tried to drive him away. This is what all good Christians do; and, therefore, temptation is to them a source of merit.

The most ordinary temptations are pride and impurity. One of the best means by which we can resist them is a life of activity for the glory of God. Many people give themselves up to idleness and indulgence; so it is not surprising that the devil has them in his power.

A religious complained to his superior of being violently tempted. The superior ordered the gardener and the cook to call him every moment. Some time after, he asked him how he was getting on. "O father," he said, "I have no time now to be tempted!"

If we were penetrated with the holy presence of God, we should find it easy to resist the enemy. With this thought, *God sees thee!* we should never sin.

There was once a good saint—I think it was St. Teresa—who complained to our Lord after having been tempted, and said to Him, "Where wert Thou then, O my most loving Jesus, during that horrible tempest?" Our Lord answered her, "I was in the midst of thy heart, taking pleasure in seeing thee fight against it."

At the moment of temptation we must firmly renew our baptismal promises. . . . Now listen well to that. When you are tempted, offer to the good God the merit of that temptation, to obtain the opposite virtue. If you are tempted to pride, offer the temptation to obtain humility; that of immodest thoughts, to obtain purity; or charity, if it is against your neighbour. Offer also the temptation to obtain the conversion of sinners; that spites the devil and puts him to flight, because the temptation is turned against himself: yes, after that he will be sure to leave you alone.

A Christian ought always to be ready for battle. As in time of war sentinels are always placed here and there to see if the enemy is approaching, so we ought to be always on our guard to see if the enemy is not laying snares for us, and if he is not coming to surprise us. One of two things: a Christian either rules his inclinations, or his inclinations rule him; there is no medium. It is like two men taking each other by the collar to try which is the strongest — one will throw the other down. One will almost always end by overthrowing the other; and when he has him on the ground, with his foot upon his neck, he does not care much for him: he has the upper hand. So with our passions; the struggle is seldom equal,— either we guide our passions, or they guide us.

My brethren, how sad it is to let ourselves be led by our passions! A Christian is noble; he ought to command his vassals like a nobleman. Our vassals are our passions. A shepherd was asked what he was. He answered, that he was a king. Over whom do you reign? Over my subjects. And who are your subjects? My inclinations. This shepherd was quite right in saying that he was a king.

We are in this world like a ship upon the sea. What causes the waves? The storm. In this world the wind is always blowing. Our passions raise a tempest in our soul; and these struggles will gain us heaven.

We must not imagine that there is any place on the earth where we could escape from this war. We shall find the devil every where; and every where he will try to deprive us of heaven. But every where and always we may be the conquerors. It is not like other battles, in which one of two parties is always beaten ; in this, if we choose, with the grace of God, which is never refused us, we may always triumph.

When we think all is lost, we have only to cry out, " O Lord, save us; we perish !" For our Lord is there, close to us, looking at us with complacency, and saying to us with a smile : " In truth thou lovest Me ; I see that thou lovest Me." It is indeed by battles against hell, and by resistance to temptations, that we give God proofs of our love.

How many souls, unknown in the world, will one day be seen enriched by these victories of every moment ! The good God will say to these souls, " Come, ye blessed of My Father, . . . enter into the joy of your Master." . . .

Our guardian angel is always there by our side, pen in hand, to write down our victories. We must say every morning, " Come, my soul, let us labour to obtain heaven. This evening our battles will be over." And in the evening, " To-morrow, my soul, all the troubles of life will perhaps be over for thee." . . .

We have not yet suffered like the martyrs. Ask them if they are sorry now . . . The good God does not require so much from us.

... There are some people who are upset by a single word. One little humiliation capsizes the ship...

Courage! my brethren, courage! when the last day comes, you will say, " Happy struggles, that have purchased heaven!"

Let us then fight generously. When once the devil sees that he has no power over us, he will leave us in peace. This is the way he usually treats sinners who are returning to God; he lets them taste the sweetness of the first moments of their conversion, because he knows very well that he would gain nothing; they are too fervent. He waits a few months, till their first ardour has passed away; then he begins to make them neglect prayer and the Sacraments; he attacks them with divers temptations; then come the battles, and then indeed is the time to ask for strength, and not to let ourselves be overcome. Some people are so weak that when they are a little tempted, they give way, like *soft paper*. If we were always marching forward like good soldiers, we should raise our hearts to God when war or temptation come upon us, and take courage. But we linger behind; we say, " Provided I am saved, that is all I want. I do not wish to be a saint." If you are not a saint, you will be lost; there is no medium—you must be one or the other; mind that. All those who will one day possess heaven will be saints. The souls in purgatory are saints, because they have no mortal sins; they have only to be purified, and they are friends of the good God. Let us work hard, my children; the day will come that we shall find we have not done at all too much to gain heaven.

IV.

HOMILY ON THE GOSPEL FOR THE TWENTY-FIRST SUNDAY AFTER PENTECOST.

O GOD, forgive us our trespasses, as we forgive them that trespass against us! The good God will forgive those who have forgiven: that is the law. There are some who carry their folly so far as not to say this part of the Lord's Prayer; as if God did not see the bottom of the heart, and paid attention only to the movements of the lips!

The saints have no hatred, no bitterness; they forgive every thing, and think they deserve much more for their offences against the good God. But bad Christians are revengeful.

The moment we hate our neighbour, God gives us back this hatred; it is an arrow which turns back against ourselves. I said one day to some one: "But then, you do not wish to go to heaven, as you will not see that man?" "Oh, yes; . . . but we shall try to keep far from each other, that we may not see each other." They will not have that trouble, for the gates of heaven are closed against hatred. In heaven there is no rancour. Good and humble hearts, who receive insults and calumnies with joy or indifference, begin their paradise in this world; and those who bear malice are unhappy,—their face is careworn, and their eyes seem ready to devour every thing.

There are people who, with a pious exterior, are offended at the smallest insult, at the least calumny. One might be such a saint as to work miracles, but if one has not charity, one will not go to heaven. A religious at the point of death, who had led an ordinary life, and had not been given to great austerities, was yet in great tranquillity. His superior expressed to him his astonishment. The religious answered him: "I have always forgotten all the evil that has been done to me; I have forgiven it with all my heart; and I hope the good God will forgive me."

The way to overcome the devil, when he excites in us thoughts of hatred against those who do us evil, is to pray immediately for their conversion.

That is the way we shall attain to overcoming evil with good, and that is what the saints do. But these Christians in appearance will not bear any thing; every thing vexes them: they answer sharp words with sharp words. When we begin to let ourselves loose, we pour out our hatred. Our heart is like a reservoir full of gall, which we are always ready to discharge upon those who are nearest to us.

It is self-love that leads us always to believe we deserve praise; while we ought to seek only for the insults that are our due. But I am innocent, you say; I do not deserve to be treated in such a way. You do not deserve it for what you have done to-day, but you deserve it for what you did yesterday. You deserve it for your other sins, and you ought to thank the good God for letting you expiate them.

The devil leaves bad Christians very quiet—nobody takes any notice of them; but against those who do good he stirs up a thousand calumnies, a thousand outrages. This is a source of great merits. . . .

In the country, where I was a curate, there was a person who occupied herself in placing out poor girls. It often happened that people came to reproach her; then she always humbled herself, took it all in good part, and made excuses. So people said of her, "Oh! as for her, she is a saint!" Indeed, saints are like that. That is true devotion. . . . It is like St. John of God, who made himself pass for a madman. When some one had written to the superior of the hospice where he was, to be careful, for that he had a saint who made himself pass for mad, the superior made apologies to him; and the saint had only one regret—that he had been recognised, and had no longer to endure the humiliations, the blows, and the disagreeable remedies adapted to his pretended malady, and under which he practised unfailing obedience.

A woman whose son had been carried off by the Moors, came to a priest to impart to him her grief. Having no means of ransoming the prisoner, the good missioner was very much embarrassed. After having reflected for a moment, he said to the poor mother: "I shall go and take the place of your child; sell me for his ransom." She was not willing; but, persuaded by the entreaties of the missioner, she consented. The child was restored to his mother, and the missioner became a slave among the Turks, who were not sparing in their ill-treatment of him. He had indeed perfect charity; he preferred his neighbour to himself. We, on the contrary, are vexed at the good fortune of others.

If one of your friends is praised, and nothing

is said of you, it makes you sad. If you see some one who has been converted, and is making rapid progress in virtue, and who has arrived in a short time at a high degree of perfection, it gives you pain to see yourself so far behind. If he is praised, you are grieved, and say, "Oh! but he was not always like that. He was just like other people. He committed such a fault, and again such a fault." All that is pride. And nothing is so contrary to charity as pride; they are fire and water.

The good Christian is very different, my children; he is compared to a dove, because he has no bitterness; he loves all men—the good because they are good, the wicked out of compassion, because he hopes by loving them to make them better, and because he sees in them souls redeemed by the Blood of Jesus Christ. He prays for sinners, and says to our Lord, "O God, do not permit those poor souls to perish!" Thus it is that we attain to heaven. While those who think they are worth something, because they keep up certain pious practices, but who are constantly a prey to jealousy and hatred, will find themselves quite unprovided at the last day.

We ought to hate nothing but the devil, sin, and ourselves.

We should have the charity of St. Augustine,

who rejoiced when he saw any very good person: "At least," he said, "there is one who will make amends to the good God for my little love."

A man of quality, in crossing a wood, met the murderer of one of his relations; he had several times promised himself revenge: when he saw him, he drew his sword. The other immediately threw himself at his feet, and said to him, "For the love of God, pardon me!" At the name of God, his enemy could not strike; he sheathed his sword again, and said, "I pardon thee." The next day he went to church, and said to the good God, "Thou wilt surely pardon me, since I have pardoned?" There was a large crucifix there, which bowed its head in token of assent.

A man who had been taken to prison, unjustly accused of stealing some cattle, was in despair. An angel appeared to him, and said to him: "It is true thou art not guilty of the theft of which thou art accused; but dost thou not remember that thou couldst have saved that man who was drowning? and thou didst not do it. It is for this thou art now suffering."

V.

HOMILY FOR THE LAST SUNDAY IN THE YEAR.

THE world passes away; we pass away with it. Kings, emperors, all go. We are swallowed up in eternity, from which we never return. There is only one thing to be done—to save our poor soul.

The saints were not attached to the goods of earth; they thought only of those of heaven. Worldly people, on the contrary, think of nothing but the present time.

A good Christian is like those who go into foreign countries to lay up money; they never think of remaining abroad, and they have nothing more at heart than to return to their own country, when once their fortune is made. Again, we should do like kings. When they are going to be dethroned, they send their treasures before them; and these treasures are waiting for them. So a good Christian sends all his good works to the gate of heaven.

The good God has placed us on the earth to see how we shall conduct ourselves, and whether we shall love Him; but no one remains on it. A man who had been condemned to the galleys for a hundred years came back from them, it is said. When he returned, every body had disappeared : he recognised nothing but the houses. . . .

If we were to reflect upon this, we should incessantly raise our eyes to heaven, our true country. But we let ourselves be carried here and there by the world, riches, and material enjoyments; and we do not give a thought to the only thing that should occupy us.

Look at the saints. How detached they were from the world and from matter! With what contempt they looked upon all these things! A religious, having lost his parents, found himself in possession of great wealth. When the news reached him, he said, " How long is it since my parents died ?" " Three weeks," they answered. " Tell me, can a person who is dead inherit property?" " Certainly not." " Well, then, I cannot inherit from those who have been dead three weeks, since I have been dead these twenty years." Ah! the saints understood the nothingness, the vanity of this world, and the happiness of giving up every thing for that bright hope of heaven!

There are two sorts of avarice : the avarice of heaven, and the avarice of earth. The miser of the earth does not carry his thoughts beyond time. He never has riches enough; he is always heaping up, heaping up. But when the moment of death comes, he will have nothing. I have often told you so; it is just like those who make too large a provision for winter, and when the next harvest comes, they do not know what to do with it: it only serves to embarrass them. We carry away nothing; we leave every thing.

What would you say of a person who should lay up in the house great stores of provisions that he would be obliged to throw away, because they would spoil; and who should neglect the precious stones, gold, and diamonds, which he might keep, and carry away with him, and which would make his fortune? . . . Well, my children, we do the same; we attach ourselves to matter, to what must come to an end; and we do not think of acquiring heaven, the only real treasure.

A good Christian, a heavenly miser, makes very little account of earthly goods; he thinks only of embellishing his soul, of laying up what will always please him, what will last for ever. Look at the kings, the emperors, the great ones of the earth: they are very rich; but are they happy? If they love the good God, they are; but if not, they are not happy. For my part, I think none are so much to be pitied as the rich when they do not love the good God.

The saints were not attached to wealth as

we are; they were attached to what will make them happy for all eternity.

Go from world to world, from kingdom to kingdom, from riches to riches, from pleasure to pleasure,—you will never find happiness. The whole earth can no more satisfy an immortal soul, than a pinch of meal can satiate a famished man.

When the Apostles had seen our Lord ascend into heaven, they found the earth without Him so dreary, so vile, so contemptible, that they sought after the tortures that would the sooner snatch them away from it, and reunite them to their good Master. The mother of the Machabees, who saw her seven children die, and who died seven times, said to them, to encourage them, "Look up to heaven." . . .

Our Lord rewarded the faith of the saints by showing heaven to their senses. Some of them have been in paradise. St. Stephen, while he was being stoned, saw heaven opened above his head. St. Paul was rapt into heaven, and declared that he could give no idea of what he had seen there. St. Teresa saw heaven, and, as she says, every thing on earth seemed to her ever after nothing but dirt.

But we, alas! are nothing but matter. We creep upon the ground, and know not how to raise ourselves on high: we are too clumsy, too heavy.

The earth is a bridge for us to pass over the water.

A bad Christian cannot understand this sweet hope of heaven, which consoles, which animates a good Christian. All that makes the happiness of the saints appears hard and difficult to him.

These are consoling thoughts, my children; with whom shall we be in heaven? With God, who is our Father; with Jesus Christ, who is our Brother; with the Blessed Virgin, who is our Mother; with the angels and saints, who are our friends.

A king, in his last moments, said with regret, "Must I, then, leave my kingdom, to go to a country where I know no one!" This was because he had never thought of the happiness of heaven. We must make friends there for ourselves now, that we may meet them again after death, and then we shall not be, like that king, afraid of knowing no one.

PART III.

CHAPTER I.

THE CURÉ OF ARS IN HIS CONVERSATION.

ONE of the great errors of our day is to imagine that piety prevents the development of the natural qualities of man; that it confines the thoughts, and is incompatible with enlightened elevation of character and warmth of feeling. Every one has heard this paradox repeated; weak Christians have believed it, and it has afflicted those of stronger faith.

It is difficult to imagine how displeasing to the ears of most worldly people are the words "devout" and "devotion." As if the finest and most noble faculties of man lost by submitting to Christian discipline, and gained by disorder! The reverse of this is the truth.

Habitual union with God by prayer and love, the continual victory of the spiritual over the material, the permanent triumph of good over evil, which we call the state of grace, is admirably reflected in the intelligent part of our being, as well and better than in the inferior part. It is the health of the soul; and putting it in possession of its object, which is

God, the Infinite, restores its beauty, its grandeur, strength, and dignity.

But is not sacrifice, it may be said, the foundation of Christian morals, and the great lesson of the Gospel? Sacrifice is precisely the law of the intellectual and moral progress of man when he is *holy;* it is the development of the most noble attributes of the soul that aspires to the glorious liberty of the children of God, and passes over all the obstacles which visible things would place in its way. It is the passage from death to life, from darkness to light, from slavery to liberty.

Till we have freely renounced every created object, by an earnest application of the doctrine of sacrifice, liberty of the soul is but a name; we are free only like a bird held by a string, which may think itself free while it does not attempt to fly, but the moment it tries to get away, perceives that it is a prisoner. Such is the liberty that attachment to creatures leaves us. "If, therefore, the Son shall make you free, you shall be free indeed."*

This love does not devastate the heart as passions do; nor does it suppress any thing which ought to remain in it. The love of Jesus Christ in the heart of man is like a ray of sun shining through the painted windows of a

* St. John viii. 36.

cathedral, colouring and embellishing it, but destroying and displacing nothing. In a soul filled with this love, strong and sweet beyond conception, the sacred fire burns the more brightly and purely for being hidden.

It is supposed that persons consecrated to God cannot possess enlightened minds or noble and generous hearts. As if human feelings were not beautified by the struggles of duty; and as if holiness did not raise the soul to a higher destiny, by releasing it from the bonds of time, and enabling it to unite itself to the Eternal Object of its love! The breaking of all bonds and the removal of all obstacles does not mean the destruction of all love and the suppression of all liberty. Fountains are not dried up by being sanctified; and holiness, far from disfiguring, elevates and purifies whatever it touches. It gives to the good dispositions which we have by nature, an increase of strength and wisdom, which is the work of the Holy Ghost.

This intellectual and moral perfection of the human faculties, refined by grace, was very striking in M. Vianney.

We are ready to allow that he had no variety or extent of human sciences. Where, when, or how could he have acquired them? But he had what supplies the place of knowledge, and even of experience—the faith which knows and foresees all things. He had great practical wisdom, a profound knowledge of the ways of God and of the miseries of man, an admirable sagacity, a prompt and accurate judgment, an acute, judicious, and penetrating mind. He was endowed, besides, with a supernatural memory, an exquisite tact, and a power of observation which would have made him formidable to those who approached him, if his great and indulgent charity had not softened all his judgments.

Out of the little unknown corner of the earth where Providence had placed him, rather under a bushel than on a candlestick, he shone before the world with incomparable brilliancy; he was a triple representation of our Lord, setting before men the light of truth, with an example of captivating goodness, and edifying virtue.

" The Curé of Ars is a holy man," some one said to a learned professor of philosophy, " but he is nothing else."

" He is enlightened," answered he, " very enlightened. He shows it in his conversations on every sort of subject, on God and on the world, on men and on things, on the present and the future. . . . Oh, how clearly and how well we see, when we see by the light of the Holy Ghost! To what heights does faith raise our intellect and our reason!"

After an interview with M. Vianney, a very distinguished man wrote as follows: " We are in admiration of the *progressive* spirit of your saint. Nothing elevates the ideas of the most humble of men like holiness!"

Although absorbed in the duties of his ministry of prayer, teaching, and direction, the Curé of Ars was indifferent to no question which, directly or indirectly, affected the interests of religion or of society. He had very clear opinions on a multitude of questions, which the cleverest people often cannot decide, but which he always solved by looking at them as they regarded the glory of God and the good of souls.

The world will perhaps say again: "But this man, who always denied himself all human pleasures, who had never known the sweetness or the benefits of social and civilised life, who so constantly and completely practised renouncement, and whose whole life was passed in the obscure enclosure of a confessional, must have taken a narrow and severe view of every thing, and his austerity could leave no room for kindness or indulgence." This is another mistake.

This man, so severe to himself, and who bore in his whole person the marks of the most terrible penance, was amiable and gentle; his conversation was sweet and refined, full of truth and consolation, and had a singular power of attraction.

In the company of priests or of Christians, whom he knew and loved, he willingly expanded; and this intimate intercourse was full of gaiety and simplicity, of tender charity, of ingenious and appropriate remarks, which went to the heart of all. These would make a delightful and admirable book ; but, unfortunately, we have not sufficient details, and if we had them, the task would be beyond our power. A smile cannot be written down, and the conversations of the Curé of Ars were as the smile of his soul. He never laughed; but that smile seldom left his lips, encouraging cheerfulness, and inspiring confidence. The Spirit of God which was in him gave an incomparable fitness and simplicity to all his words, which were animated by the extreme tenderness of his heart. We might gather up his least words.

Thus, the good Curé long lamented Mademoiselle d'Ars, and always retained a tender veneration for her memory. When he paid his first visit to the new inhabitants of the Castle, he expressed his regret before them, saying, "Poor lady ! how sad it is to see her no more on her poor bench in church !" . . . Then, fearing he might have been wanting in delicacy to the heir of his benefactress, he suddenly reproached himself for his sorrow and his tears, adding, "And yet . . . we are wrong to complain. The good God treats us as He treated His people. When he took away Moses, he left them Caleb and Josue."

A little while after, in returning their good wishes for the new year, he said to the family which was soon to take its place in his heart next to Mademoiselle d'Ars, "I should like to be St. Peter, and I would give you the keys of paradise for a new-year's gift." Once when they had presented to him some of their numerous relations, and asked for a special blessing upon them, the holy Curé gave it, saying, "Oh! the cousins of M. des. Garets are already blessed!"

When Mgr. de Langalerie in one of his frequent visits, said to him, "My good Curé, will you permit me to celebrate Holy Mass in your church?" he answered, "Monseigneur, I am sorry it is not Christmas, that you might say three."

The first time Père Hermann came to Ars, they wanted him to preach, and the good Curé asked him to catechise the crowd instead of him. The Rev. Father took good care not to accept the offer; he only consented to say a few words after the servant of God had spoken—and even that was a great deal for his humility. M. Vianney gave his instruction as usual, and ended it thus : " My children, there was once a good saint who wished very much to hear the Blessed Virgin sing. Our Lord, who takes pleasure in doing the will of those who love Him, deigned to grant him this favour. He saw a beautiful lady, who began to sing before him. He had never heard so sweet a voice. He was ravished with delight, and cried out, 'It is enough! it is enough! if you go on, I shall die!' The beautiful lady said to him, 'Be not in a hurry to admire my singing, for what thou hast heard is nothing. I am only the virgin Catherine, and thou art going to hear the Mother of God;' and the Blessed Virgin sang in her turn. And that song was so beautiful, so beautiful, that the saint fainted and fell dead with delight . . . drowned in the balm of love ! . . . Well, my children, it will be the same thing to-day, . . . you have just heard St. Catherine; you are going to hear the Blessed Virgin."

One day a missionary recently admitted into the Society was presented to M. Vianney, and it was observed that he was the youngest of all. "You are very fortunate, my friend," said he, embracing him; "you will have more time to serve the Divine Master. In the College of the Apostles, our Lord had a tender predilection for St. James the Less, because he was the youngest."

The same missionary having gone to assist at the processions of Corpus Christi at Lyons, the Curé said to him on his return, " There was once a saint who used to disappear on the eve of all the great feasts. He was seen no more till the day after. He went to celebrate the feast in paradise. I think, my dear companion, you do like him." . . .

Wishing to show his companions in labour his esteem for their services, he said, " The good God gives me white bread to eat at the end of my days. He knows that poor old people require soft food. . . . He treats me as our Lord treated the bridegroom at the marriage-feast of Cana; he gives me the good wine at the last."

M. Vianney wished to pay for the crosses which the missionaries receive when they pronounce their vows : " Let me alone," he said ; "I have so many crosses, I can share them with my friends."

After a sermon which had pleased him, he took both the hands of the preacher in his own, saying, " Ah! our vessels were too small to hold such beautiful things ! "

A Lazarist of Valfleury asked the Curé of Ars if one of their Fathers, lately seized with paralysis, would be able to preach again. " Yes, my friend," he answered, " he will always preach. The sermons of saints are their examples."

A Parisian had said, "Sister Rosalie was my mother, and the Curé of Ars is my father." "Alas! poor orphan!" said M. Vianney, with a sigh; "the father can never replace the mother."

On the return of his missionary after a long absence, he received him with open arms, and cried out, "Ah! my friend, there you are! what happiness! I have often thought that the reprobate must be very wretched at being separated from the good God, since we suffer so much in the absence of those we love!"

An ecclesiastic was excusing himself for not having brought a surplice to assist at the High Mass on Sunday; M. Vianney reassured him, saying, "Oh, never mind. You wear it on your heart, by the whiteness of your soul."

A little child gave him a nosegay on his birthday; "My little one," he said, smiling graciously, "your nosegay is very beautiful, but your soul is still more beautiful."

One day within the Octave of Corpus Christi, the holy Curé having gone to see the magnificent preparations for the procession which were made at the Castle, they were regretting that a high wind would prevent the illumination. Pointing to the young children round the steps of the throne prepared for our Lord, he said, " These are bright and burning torches, which cannot be extinguished by the wind." And on going away, after rejoicing the hearts of all by his presence, he added, " The inhabitants of this house change, generations succeed each other; but it is ever the house of the good God." After the procession, which was very long, they wanted him to take some refreshment; he refused, saying, " It is of no use ; I want nothing. How could I be fatigued ? I was bearing Him who bears me."

During the inundations of May 1856, it happened one night that the pilgrims who were waiting in the church had bolted the door on the inside. At one o'clock in the morning, the Curé came up and knocked gently at the door; they did not hear him. He knocked again. The rain was falling in torrents ; he stood in it for some minutes, and went into the confessional without thinking any more about it. When he came into the sacristy to vest for Mass, they perceived that his cassock was dripping wet : they pressed him to change it; they asked him a thousand questions. He only answered joyously, " Let it alone, let it alone ! it is nothing ; it proves that I am not made of sugar."

M. Vianney was once making his round of visits to the sick under a burning July sun.

The priest who accompanied him, seeing his head uncovered, offered him his hat. "You would do better, my friend," said the holy Curé, "to offer me your science and your virtues." This was what you exposed yourself to by offering him any civility. It was very different if you attempted to pay him a compliment.

"How happy you are to be young!" said he to some one. "Without reckoning any thing else, you have so much strength and so much zeal to spend in the service of the good God."

"Monsieur le Curé," replied the other, "you are younger than I."

"Yes, my friend, in virtue."

"Monsieur le Curé," a person said to him another time, "since you love your missionaries, you will leave them the mantle of Elias when you depart?"

"My friend, you should not ask a mantle of him who has not even a shirt."

Speaking of that mozetta, which was a touching kindness on the part of the Bishop, but a great humiliation to the good Curé, some one observed that he was the only Canon created by Mgr. Chalandon. M. Vianney perceived the trap laid for him, and replied quickly, "I can well believe it. The Bishop was unlucky. . . He has seen his mistake, and he dares not try again."

One day he saw one of his portraits, at the foot of which were awkwardly represented his mozetta and his cross of honour. "To make it complete," he said, "they should write under it, *vanity, pride, and nothingness.*"

Another time, allusion was made to these different dignities. "Yes," answered he, "I am an honorary Canon by the kindness of the Bishop, a knight of the Legion of Honour by a mistake of the government, and . . . the shepherd of three sheep and an ass by the will of my father."

One day, the Curé of Ars saw a person come into the sacristy whom it was easy to recognise by his appearance and language as a man of the world. The stranger approached him respectfully; and the servant of God, thinking he knew what he came for, pointed to the little stool on which his penitents were accustomed to kneel.

The fine gentleman, who perfectly understood the gesture, hastened to say, "M. le Curé, I am not come for confession; I am come to reason with you."

"O my friend, you have come to the wrong person; I cannot reason; . . . . . but if you are in want of consolation, place yourself there" (and he again pointed inexorably to the stool), "and be assured that many others have done so before you, and have not repented of it."

"But, M. le. Curé, I have already had the honour of telling you that I did not come for confession, and that for a decisive reason—I have no faith. I believe no more in confession than in any thing else."

"You have no faith, my friend? Oh, how I pity you! You live in a mist. . . . . A little child who knows its catechism knows more than you. I thought myself very ignorant; but you are still more so. . . You have no faith? Well, place yourself there, and I will hear your confession. When you have made your confession, you will believe just as I do."

"But, M. le Curé, it is neither more nor less than a comedy that you are advising me to act with you."

"Place yourself there, I tell you!"

The persuasion, the sweetness, the tone of authority tempered by grace, with which these words were spoken, induced this man to fall on his knees, almost in spite of himself. He made the sign of the cross, which he had long disused, and began the humble acknowledgment of his faults. He arose not only consoled, but fully believing, having experienced that the shortest and surest road to faith is to do the works of faith, according to the eternal word of the Divine Master, "He that doth the truth cometh to the light."

The founder of a celebrated orphanage consulted M. Vianney on the opportunity of obtaining the attention and the patronage of the public, through the medium of the press. " Instead of making a noise in the newspapers," answered the servant of God, " make a noise at the door of the tabernacle."

" M. le Curé," replied this good man, " I should be very glad to make my novitiate with you."

" Do not be uneasy; they will give you one," replied M. Vianney, alluding to the trials which awaited the new foundation.

A postulant, who had just left the Congregation of the Sisters of St. Vincent of Paul, one day had an interview at Ars with a priest lately arrived from Jerusalem, who told M. Vianney that he had advised her to go to the East, to employ her strength and her zeal in those parts. The good Curé, who was aware of her fickleness, answered, " Send her to paradise. There *at least* she will not wish for change."

We may see that M. Vianney was ready with quick answers, which were now and then gently malicious.

" M. le Curé," said a person whose broad

face and robust appearance contrasted singularly with the paleness and emaciation of the holy old man, " I reckon on you to take me up to heaven. I hope you do not forget your friends, and that you give me a good share of the merit of your fasts and penances. When you go to heaven, I shall try to take hold of your cassock."

"O my friend, take good care not to do that," replied the good Curé. "The gate of heaven is narrow,"—and he cast a little malicious glance at the broad shoulders of the other,—" we should both remain outside at the gate."

He was afraid he might have hurt the feelings of his visitor by these words, though they were spoken in joke, and in the kindest manner; and he made the most humble and polite excuses for them.

A religious said to him with simplicity, "You are generally thought ignorant, Father." "They are right, my daughter; but it is no matter, for I will tell you more than you will do."

He was asked for some relics for a person who was very desirous of having them. He replied, smiling, "Let her make some!"

One of his parishioners, an excellent girl, full of zeal and devotedness, but whose zeal was sometimes too eager and impetuous, like that of the Apostles before Pentecost, wanted to give him advice : " M. le Curé, you are wrong in doing this ; you ought to do that." . . . " Come," interrupted the holy man gently, " we are not yet in England," alluding to the English constitution, which allows a woman to be at the head of the government.

M. Vianney was often mirthful.

Brother Athanasius, the director of the school of Ars, returning from a drive, was relating how his horse had started and thrown him into the ditch. The good Curé condoled with him on the accident, and then added : " My friend, St. Antony never fell out of a carriage ; you should do like him." " M. le Curé, how did St. Antony do ?" " He went always on foot."

M. Vianney could give answers that were irresistibly convincing. A freethinker one day declared to him that there were some things in religion which it was impossible for him to believe.

" For example— ?" said the good Curé.

" For example, the eternity of punishment."

" My friend, I advise you never to speak of religion."

" And why not ?"

" Because you should first learn your catechism. What does the catechism say ? That we must believe the Gospel, because it is the word of our Lord. Do you believe the Gospel?"

"Yes, M. le Curé."

"Well, the Gospel says, 'Depart into everlasting fire!' What more would you have? That appears to me sufficiently clear."

The Curé of Ars had an interview one day with a rich Protestant. The servant of God did not know that he had the misfortune to belong to a sect, and spoke to him, as he was accustomed to do, of our Lord and the saints with the warmest effusion, ending by putting a medal into his hand. The other said, on receiving it:

"M. le Curé, you are giving a medal to a heretic—at least, I am a heretic only from your point of view. Notwithstanding the difference of our belief, I hope we shall both be one day in heaven."

The good Curé took his hand, and fixing on him his eyes, which expressed his lively faith and his burning charity, he said, in a tone of deep compassion and tenderness: "Alas, my friend, we shall be united above only inasmuch as we have begun to be so upon earth; death will make no change. Where the tree falls, there it lies."

"M. le Curé, I trust in Christ, who said, 'He ho believeth in Me shall have eternal life.'"

"Ah! my friend, our Lord also said other things. He said that whoever would not listen to the Church should be regarded as a heathen. He said that there was to be but one flock and one shepherd, and He appointed St. Peter to be the head of that flock." Then, speaking in a more gentle and insinuating voice, "My friend, there are not two ways of serving our Lord—there is only one good way; and it is to serve Him as He wishes to be served."

Thereupon the good Curé disappeared, leaving that man penetrated with a salutary uneasiness, the forerunner of divine grace, by which he was afterwards happily overcome.

Notwithstanding his decided love of solitude, M. Vianney's disposition was open, and his conversation at once flowing and reserved. To avoid remarks painful to his humility, he never asked questions, nor allowed time for others to ask them; he kept the lead in conversation, and seemed afraid of having a reply. He had not the shadow of self-love, and if he spoke occasionally of himself, it was because his humility urged him to it, and the power of opening his heart seemed to be a support to his weakness. Not being able to speak freely to every one, he relieved himself by confiding his thoughts to a few hearts that he could trust; and the subject of these confidences was always what most frightened and humbled him. He never revealed his whole interior; he led you to the door of his soul, and no further.

"O my God! how happy we shall be in paradise, since even already on earth the company of the saints is so delightful, and their conversation so full of charms and sweetness!" This exclamation often escaped us on coming out from those evening conversations, when the missioners of Ars had the great privilege of being admitted in turns to enjoy the intimacy of the servant of God. We felt that it was one of the rarest favours of Providence, and we showed our appreciation of it by words and by tears, but most often by a religious silence.

The end of those long and fatiguing days was the time when he talked with most familiarity, warmth, and freedom. Standing at the corner of the fire-place, or before his little table, according as his benumbed limbs required the warmth of the fire, with a beaming, happy countenance, the joy and innocence of his soul showed itself in a thousand sparkling remarks, full of similes and of sweetness.

Following the counsel of St. Paul, he avoided vain and profane discourse, and idle questions which lead to controversy rather than to edification. If any little debate arose before him, he modestly kept silence, as if he were afraid of disobliging either party by giving an opinion. If he was asked, he put in a gracious and conciliatory word, or laid down one of those great principles which are beyond discussion, and which restore peace between adversaries, by bringing them into ground where dispute is no longer possible.

His soul was always soaring like an angelic being above the strife of vulgar interests and passions. He looked at every thing from that point of view, familiar to the saints, where dwells light without shadow. Conscience was his only horizon. The exterior world had no place in his mind.

Nothing was good or pleasant or interesting in his eyes but what related to the good God. The heart is where the treasure is. The Sovereign Good attracted him to such a degree that he could not turn his thoughts elsewhere. His conversation was more divine than human, and breathed the perfume of heaven. He spoke of the mysteries of the other world as if he had come back from it, and of the vanities of this world with a gentle irony that made you smile. As he went on speaking, he became more at his ease, and the warmth of his soul diffused itself more freely.

If any troublesome person,—for there was a great variety among the pilgrims who came to him,—if any troublesome and indiscreet person came to talk of worldly affairs, however important they might be, the holy Curé was too kind and too civil to interrupt him, but he was silent, and visibly annoyed. But these cases were rare, for he was surrounded by a sort of divine atmosphere, which kept people from introducing worldly topics, for fear of disturbing its purity.

In this age of activity, novelty, and progress, in these laborious and disturbed times, the Curé of Ars had no desire whatever to know any thing about this world, nor did he pay the least attention to passing events ; so completely had he come to use things as not using them, to enjoy them as not enjoying them ; his whole mind and heart being bent on another object.

" You speak sometimes of the railway, M. le Curé," some one said to him ; " do you know what it is ?"

" No, and I do not wish to know ; I speak of it because I hear others speak of it."

This man, to whom the railways every day brought from two to three hundred strangers, died without having ever seen a railway, or having any idea what it was like.

But if he was a stranger to every thing belonging to the material world, he found infinite delight and consolation in every thing that belonged to the divine world,—that is, the Church of Jesus Christ, the kingdom of souls bought and redeemed by His Blood; in all that increased His glory, that tended to the diffusion of His doctrine, to the triumph of truth; that multiplied the number of the faithful destined to praise Him for ever.

However sublime might be the subject of the conversation, the good Curé always preserved that simplicity which is the true characteristic of the children of God. In speaking of the saints, of heaven, and of divine things, he kept his familiar language, and used popular comparisons. The charms of divine love, the delights of the Eucharist, the happiness of the good, the misery of the wicked, the expectation of eternal joys, were mingled with noble solicitude for the increase of the Kingdom of Jesus Christ, the exaltation of Holy Church, and the triumph of justice and truth.

Chapter II.

FAITH OF M. VIANNEY.

The Curé of Ars had received the gift of faith in an eminent degree. The Holy Spirit shed so bright a light on his innermost soul, that he saw divine things with a clearness, certainty, and sweetness, which caused ecstasies and tears, and the ready acquiescence of his mind in the truths that were shown to him. His intimate union with God had rendered these truths, as it were, sensible and palpable to him. What we perceive from a distance, vaguely, confusedly, through a cloud, he saw with a clear and steady eye.

"If we loved our Lord, we should have that gilded Tabernacle, that abode of the good God, always before the eyes of our mind. When we see the tower of a church on our way, the sight of it should make our heart beat, as the heart of the spouse beats at the sight of the dwelling of her beloved. We ought to be unable to take our eyes off it."

"We have nothing but a faith three hundred miles distant from its object, as if the good God were beyond the seas. If we had a lively, penetrating faith, as the saints had, we should, like them, see our Lord. *Some priests see Him every day at Mass.*" . . . Do not these words recall those of St. Paul, *Novi hominem?*

"Those who have no faith are much more blind than those who have no eyes. . . . . We are in this world like people in a thick fog; but faith is the wind which disperses it, and which causes a beautiful sun to shine on our souls.

...... See how all is sad and cold among Protestants! it is a long winter. With us all is cheerful, joyous, and consoling."

"Let worldly people talk as they please. Alas! how should they see? they are blind. Our Lord Jesus Christ might work all the miracles now that He worked in Judea, and they would not believe. He to whom all power was given has not yet lost His power. For example, last week a poor vine-dresser brought here on his shoulders a little boy of twelve years old, who was quite a cripple, and had never been able to walk. This good man made a novena to St. Philomena, and his little boy was cured the ninth day, and went away galloping before him."

"Formerly our Lord made the lame walk, healed the sick, raised the dead to life. Some people who were present then, and saw these prodigies with their own eyes, yet did not believe. Men are the same at all times and in all places. If the good God is powerful, the devil also has his power; and he makes use of it to blind the eyes of the poor world."

Chapter III.

HOPE OF M. VIANNEY.

ALTHOUGH still kept down by the bonds of the body, the Curé of Ars was scarcely less absorbed in God than those pure intelligences which ever burn before Him in the light of eternal charity. The fear of the judgments of God was his predominant idea, and despair was his temptation; nevertheless, he desired and longed for death: "It is the union," he said, "of the soul with the Sovereign Good." He often spoke of writing a book on "the delights of death." While others require all their strength to resign themselves to die, M. Vianney's effort was to resign himself to live. In his conversation, he sometimes echoed the desire of St. Paul to be soon delivered from the tabernacle of his body, that what was mortal in him might be swallowed up by life.

His most graceful comparisons related to the desire of heaven. He often made use of that of the swallow, which only skims the ground and scarcely ever alights upon it; of the flame always tending upwards; of the balloon, which rises in the air as soon as the cords that hold it down are cut. He said:

"The heart is drawn towards what it loves most: the proud to honours, the avaricious to riches; the vindictive thinks of his revenge, the immodest of his wicked pleasures. But what does the good Christian think of? Towards what will his heart turn? Towards heaven, where God is, who is his treasure."

"Man was created for heaven; the devil has broken the ladder by which he reached it. Our Lord has made another for us by His Passion; He has opened the door. The Blessed Virgin is at the top of the ladder, holding it with both her hands, and calling to us, 'Come, come!' Oh, what a beautiful invitation! What a beautiful destiny has man! To see God, to love Him, to bless Him, to contemplate Him throughout eternity!"

"When we think of heaven, can we have any regard for the earth?"

"After she had been in heaven, St. Teresa could look no more at the things here below. When she was shown any beautiful object, she said, 'That is nothing; it is only dirt.'"

"St. Colette sometimes left her cell, beside herself with joy at the thoughts of heaven, and went through the corridors crying out, 'To paradise! to paradise!'"

"In heaven our heart will be so lost, so drowned in the happiness of loving God, that we shall not be occupied with ourselves nor with others, but with God alone."

"A good Christian ought not to be able to endure himself in this world; he languishes on earth. If a little child were down there in the church, and its mother was in the tribune, it would stretch out its little arms to her; and if it could not get up the staircase leading to her, it would ask for help, and would not rest till it was in its mother's arms."

"It is said that in heaven we shall be upon thrones, to signify that we shall be great. These thrones are formed by the love of God; there is nothing else in heaven. . . The love of God will fill and inundate every thing." . . .

"When St. Teresa was asked what she had seen in heaven, she cried out, 'I have seen! I have seen! . . . I have seen!' . . . . She stopped there; breath and words failed her: she could say no more."

"Oh, the beautiful union of the Church on earth with the Church in heaven! As St. Teresa said, 'You triumphing, and we fighting, we are but one in glorifying God!'"

"St. Augustine says that he who fears death does not love God; that is very true. If you had been long separated from your father, would you not be happy to see him again?"

"Oh, what a beautiful acquisition is heaven!

But what is necessary that we may attain to it? Purity of heart, contempt of the world, and love of God."

After he had given an enchanting instruction on heaven, the Curé of Ars was asked, "What is required that we may merit this recompense, of which you have given us so magnificent a picture?" "My friend," he answered, " grace and the Cross."

He was very fond of relating this story:

"There was once a good religious, who thought he should find the time long in paradise. The good God showed him plainly that he was mistaken. One day he was in the gardens of the monastery, and perceived a little bird hopping from branch to branch, which seemed more and more beautiful as he looked at it. At last, it was so very beautiful that the monk could not take his eyes off it; he began to pursue it, and wanted to catch it. However, he stopped, thinking he must have been half an hour running after his bird. He returned to the monastery, but was very much surprised to find at the door a brother whom he had never seen, and the brother did not know him either; his surprise was still greater, when he saw nothing in the house but strange faces and new people. He said, 'And our fathers, where are they?' The others looked at him in astonishment. At last he told them his name; and they looked in the registers, and found that it was a hundred years since he went away. . . . Thus the good God showed him that the time does not seem long in paradise."

Chapter IV.

CHARITY OF M. VIANNEY.

To give an idea of M. Vianney's love of our Lord, we should have to depict all the ardour, energy, sweetness, strength, and generosity that can be concentrated in a human soul with the aid of grace. All the faculties of his mind, all the powers of his reason, all the resources of his will, were at the service of this dominant feeling. The union of which St. John Chrysostom speaks was already begun in him; Jesus Christ alone was in all his thoughts, his affections, and his desires. Without the Saviour, the society of the blessed could not have pleased him. Jesus Christ was his life, his heaven, his present, his future; and the adorable Eucharist alone could allay the thirst that consumed him. He could not cease to think of Jesus Christ, to aspire to Him, to speak of Him. Then it was not words, but flames that issued from his heart and his mouth. He pronounced the adorable name of Jesus, and said, " Our Lord," with an emphasis which could not fail to strike every one; his heart seemed to be on his lips.

What his reading had most strongly impressed on his memory, and what recurred most often in his discourses, were the burning words by which the love of the saints for the Divine Master is the most vividly expressed; he liked to quote those words of our Lord to St. Teresa : " I am waiting for the Day of Judgment to make known to men how much thou hast loved Me." And again : " When men will not have Me, I will come and hide Myself in thy heart." He never quoted them without being interrupted by his tears.

He repeated also those words of St. Catherine of Siena, who cried out in her ardour, " O my dearest Lord ! if I had been the stones and the earth where Thy Cross was planted, what grace and consolation I should have felt in receiving the Blood which flowed from Thy Wounds!" He related, with much emotion, that St. Colette said to our Lord, " My sweet Master, I desire indeed to love Thee, but my heart is too little." She then saw descend a great heart all in flames, and at the same time heard a voice saying to her, " Love Me now as much as thou wouldst." And her heart was inundated with love.

"O Jesus!" he often cried out, with his eyes full of tears, "to know Thee is to love Thee! .... If we knew how much our Lord loves us, we should die of joy! I do not believe there are any hearts so hard as not to love, when they see themselves so much loved .... Charity is so beautiful! it is an emanation from the heart of Jesus, who is all love ..... The only happiness we have on earth, is to love God, and to know that God loves us." ....

He also said, mournfully:

"I sometimes think that few good works will be rewarded, because, instead of doing them for the love of God, we do them from habit, by routine, from self-love. .... What a pity it is!"

"All in God's sight, all with God, all to please God. . . . Oh, how beautiful it is! Come, my soul, thou shalt converse with the good God, labour with Him, walk with Him, fight and suffer with Him. Thou wilt labour, but He will bless thy work; thou wilt walk, but He will bless thy footsteps; thou wilt suffer, but He will bless thy tears. How great, how noble, how consoling it is, to do every thing under the eyes and in the company of the good God! To think that He sees all, that He takes account of all. Let us say every morning, 'All to please Thee, O my God! all my actions with Thee!'.... How sweet and consoling is the thought of the presence of God!.... One is never weary; the hours slip away like minutes..... In short, it is a foretaste of heaven."

"Poor sinners! when I think that there are some who will die without having even tasted for one hour the happiness of loving God!..... When we are tired of our exercises of piety, and conversation with God wearies us, let us go to the gates of hell, and look at those poor lost souls, who can no longer love the good God. If we could lose our souls without making our Lord suffer! but we cannot."

"A Christian who had faith would die of love..... A good Christian who loves God and his neighbour,—and when we love God, we love our neighbour,—see how happy he is! What peace is in his soul!. It is paradise on earth."

"I often think that the tongue of those poor dead, who are in the cemetery yonder, can no longer pray,..... that their heart can no longer love."....

He often ended his discourse with these words: "To be loved by God, to be united to God; to live in the presence of God, to live for God; oh, beautiful life, ... and beautiful death!"

One day, when he heard the birds in his courtyard, he said, sighing, " Poor little birds ! you were created to sing, and you sing..... Man was created to love God, and he does not love Him !"

"The reason why we do not love God," he said again, " is that we have not come to the point when whatever costs us something gives us pleasure. If we had to lose our souls, it would be a consolation to be able to say, ' At least I loved the good God upon earth.' .... There are some who weep because they do not love God ; but those people love Him. Oh, how consoling it is to think that on this poor earth it is for the good God that there is most fidelity and most love !"

The Curé of Ars especially recommended three devotions : devotion to the Passion of our Lord and to the Holy Eucharist ; devotion to the Blessed Virgin ; and devotion to the souls in purgatory. He affirmed, after St. Bernard, that it was a mark of reprobation not to have a devotion to the Body and Blood of Jesus Christ. "The Passion of our Lord," he said, "is like a great river flowing down from a mountain, which is never exhausted."

It would be impossible to give an idea of his devotion to the Blessed Sacrament. He called It by the most sweet and tender names ; he invented new expressions to speak of It worthily; it was his favourite subject, and he was always recurring to It in his conversations. Then his heart melted with gratitude, happiness, and love; his eyes sparkled, his saintly soul shone forth in his countenance, and his voice was choked with tears: "What is our Lord doing in the Sacrament of His love? He assumed His good Heart that He might love us, and out of that Heart there issues a flood of mercy and tenderness to drown the sins of the world."

He called Holy Communion "a bath of love." "When we have communicated," he said, "the soul revels in the balm of love like bees among flowers."

He liked to relate the anecdote of St. John of the Cross and St. Teresa. When she received Holy Communion from her spiritual father, "the love of our Lord, passing from one to the other, melted their hearts, so that St. John of Avila fell down on one side, and St. Teresa on the other, overwhelmed by the sweetness of love."

On the Feast of the Sacred Heart, he said: "To-day our Lord places us on His Heart. . . . Ah! if we could remain there always!" . . . Then, clasping his hands and raising his eyes, full of tears, to heaven, he cried, "O Heart of Jesus! Heart of love! flower of love! . . . . .

The heart was all that remained whole in the most holy body of our Lord, after Longinus had pierced it to draw forth love. If we do not love the Heart of Jesus, what then shall we love? There is nothing in that Heart but love! How is it possible not to love what is so amiable?"

Chapter V.

THOUGHTS OF M. VIANNEY ON THE JOYS OF THE INTERIOR LIFE.

The Curé of Ars was once speaking of the joys of prayer and of the interior life; it was a subject which he never approached without his heart being immediately melted:

"To be a king," he said, "what a poor position! a king is only for men! . . . but to be for God, to be wholly for God! To be for God without reserve; our body for God, our soul for God! . . . A chaste body, a pure soul! Oh, there is nothing so beautiful!" and tears stifled his voice.

"Prayer is the only happiness of man upon earth. O beautiful life! beautiful union of the soul with our Lord! Eternity will not be long enough to comprehend this happiness. . . . The interior life is a bath of love into which the soul is plunged ; . . . it is, as it were, drowned in love ! . . . . . God holds the interior man as a mother holds the head of her child in her hands, to cover it with kisses and caresses." . . . . .

" I often think of the joy of the Apostles when they saw our Lord again. The separation had been so cruel ! Our Lord loved them so much ! He was so good to them ! We may presume that He embraced them when He said to them, ' Peace be with you !' So He embraces our soul when we pray. He says to us also, ' Peace be with you !' "

" We love a thing in proportion to what it has cost us. You may judge by that of our Lord's love for our soul, which has cost Him all His Blood. He is eager for communications and intercourse with it. He longs to see it, to hear it." . . . .

" There are two ways of uniting ourselves with our Lord and of saving our souls : prayer and the Sacraments. All those who have become saints have frequented the Sacraments, and have raised their souls to God by prayer. We ought in the morning on awaking, to offer to God our heart, our mind, our thoughts, our words, our actions, our whole selves, to serve for His glory alone. We should renew our baptismal vows, thank our guardian angel, ask for the protection of that good angel who has remained by our side during our sleep."

" Some good Christians are in the habit of saying, ' I will make so many acts of the love of God, so many sacrifices to-day;' . . . . I like that practice very much." . . .

" We should often, in the course of the day, ask for the light of the Holy Ghost. Oh, how much we stand in need of it, that we may know our poor misery! We should say a *Pater* and *Ave* for the conversion of sinners, for the souls in purgatory; . . . . . and often repeat, ' O my God, have pity on me!' like a child saying to its mother, ' Give me a bit of bread ; . . . give me your hand ; . . . . embrace me!' " . . .

" He who does not pray is like a hen or a turkey that cannot rise into the air. If they fly a little, they soon fall down, and, scratching a hole in the earth, they nestle in it, cover their heads with dust, and seem to have no other pleasure. He who prays, on the contrary, is like an intrepid eagle, which soars in the air, and seems always to wish to approach nearer to the sun. Such is the good Christian on the wings of prayer. Oh, how beautiful is prayer! The man who is in favour with God does not require to be taught to pray; he knows naturally how to pray, because he knows his own wants."

" Union with Jesus Christ, union with the

Cross : that is salvation. Love is the distinctive mark of the elect, as the mark of the reprobate is hatred. No reprobate loves another reprobate ; the brother detests his brother, the son his father, the mother her child ; and this universal hatred is concentrated upon God : this is hell." " The saints love every one ; above all, they love their enemies. . . . . . Their heart, inflamed with divine love, dilates itself in proportion to the number of souls that the good God puts in their way, as the wings of the hen extend in proportion to the number of her young ones." " The heart of the saints is as steadfast as a rock in the midst of the sea."

" Those persons who practise devotion, who go often to confession and communion, and who fail to do works of faith and charity, are like trees in blossom. You think there will be as much fruit as flower ; but there is a great difference." . . . .

" Oh, how beautiful will be the day of the resurrection ! we shall see those beautiful souls come from heaven, like suns of glory, and unite themselves to the bodies which they animated on earth. The more those bodies have been mortified, the more they will shine like diamonds."

" None are really miserable but bad Christians, who forsake prayer and the Sacraments, and wallow in sin; for good Christians feel no misfortunes. . . . To possess God, that is the joy of joys. That happiness makes us forget all else. Like that good saint whose life I was reading, who remained in ecstasy from Shrove-Tuesday till Easter-Day, he returned to his senses just in time for the Resurrection. . . . . That happiness also makes us forget sufferings. . . . Once the wind carried away the bear-skin with which St. Simeon was covered. When people saw that he did not stir upon his column, they went up, and they found him frozen. They plunged him into warm water to revive him: 'Why did you not leave me alone?' he said; 'I was so happy.'"

"To pray well, we need not speak much. We know that the good God is there, in the holy Tabernacle; we open our heart, we take pleasure in His holy presence; that is the best sort of prayer." "Like the good M. de Vidaud; he used to rise very early in the morning, and go to adore the Blessed Sacrament as soon as the church was open. One day, when he was at a country house, they were obliged to send three times to the chapel to fetch him to break-fast; the mistress of the house grew impatient. At the third message, he came away from the presence of our Lord, saying, 'O my God, can one not remain, then, a moment in peace with

Thee!'" The Curé of Ars added, weeping, " He had been there since four o'clock in the morning ! There are some good Christians who would thus pass their whole lives absorbed in adoration before God. Oh, how happy they are !"

One day, when he had been presiding over the renewal of vows which the Sisters of St. Joseph are accustomed to make every year on the 2d of July, M. Vianney came out from the ceremony with a full heart, unable to contain his joy; he gave utterance to it in sweet words : " How lovely is religion !" he said. " How great is the multitude of Thy sweetness, O my God, to them that fear Thee ! . . . I was thinking just now, that between our Lord and those good religious there was a strife of generosity, who should give the most. . . . But our Lord always wins. The religious give Him their heart, and He gives His Heart and His Body. . . . While the Sisters said, 'I renew my vows of povery, chastity, and obedience,' I said to them as I presented the Host, 'May the Body of our Lord keep your soul for life everlasting !'" Then, taking occasion to dilate upon his beloved subject, he added :

" If we could but comprehend all the blessings that are contained in Holy Communion, nothing more would be required to satisfy the heart of man. The avaricious would no longer run after treasures, nor the ambitious after glory; every one would forsake the earth, would shake off its dust, and take flight towards heaven. Communion! Oh, what honour God does to His creature! He reposes on his tongue, passes over his palate as over a little road, and stays in his heart as upon a throne! O my God! my God! some people have known how to appreciate this honour. Thus, a holy Bishop has been known to sweep the church himself, and to put on his rochet for this function, which appears degrading, but which he esteemed so highly that he wore his insignia of a Bishop to perform it. A king used formerly to press the grapes with his own hands for the consecration of the Chalice, and to prepare the flour for the Hosts."

"One Communion well made is sufficient to inflame the soul with the love of God, and to make it despise the earth. It is not long since a great person of this world came here to go to Holy Communion; he had a fortune of three hundred thousand francs: he gave a hundred to build a church, a hundred to the poor, a hundred to his relations, and went to La Trappe. After him there came a very learned lawyer; he made a good Communion, and set out to go and put himself into the hands of Père Lacordaire. Oh! one Holy Communion, one alone, is enough to disgust a man with the earth, and to give him a foretaste of heavenly delights!"

"One ought to be a seraphim to say Mass! .... I hold our Lord in my hands. I put Him on the right, and He remains on the right! I put Him on the left, and He remains on the left! ..... If we knew what Holy Mass is, we should die! We shall never, till we are in heaven, understand the happiness of saying Mass! Alas! my God! how much is a priest to be pitied, when he does it as if he were doing an ordinary action!" . . . . .

Chapter VI.

ZEAL OF M. VIANNEY.

ONE evening, the servant of God appeared more overpowered with fatigue than usual; he had nearly fainted during the short walk from his confessional to the presbytery. His ideas of flight and retirement came upon him again, but they did not prevent him from being as gay, as amiable and open as usual, and even more so. "Oh!" said he, taking his missionary by both hands, "if I were in your place, I would fly away to heaven!" Then, with great sadness and in a sorrowful voice, "How much am I to be pitied! I know nobody more unhappy than I am!"

"M. le Curé, how many people would like to change with you!"

"My friend, they would exchange their gold for copper."

"O my God!" he often said, "how long I find the time among sinners! When, then, shall I be with the saints! . . The good God is so much offended on the earth, that one would be tempted to ask for the end of the world! We could not endure this life if there were not a few beautiful souls to give repose to our heart, and to console our eyes for all the evil that we see and hear. . . . . When we think of the ingratitude of man to the good God, we are tempted to go to the other end of the world to avoid seeing it. It is frightful! And then if the good God were not so good! But He is so good!" . . . .

"O God! how ashamed shall we be, when the day of the last judgment shall show us our ingratitude! We shall understand then, but it will be too late. Our Lord will say to us, 'Why hast thou offended Me?' And we shall not know what to answer."

"No, there is nothing in the world so unhappy as a priest! In what is his life passed? In seeing the good God offended. Always His holy Name blasphemed! Always His commandments broken! Always His love outraged! The priest sees nothing else; he hears nothing else. . . . . . He is continually, like St. Peter in the judgment-hall of Pilate, having before his eyes our Lord insulted, despised, mocked, covered with ignominy. . . . . Some spit in His face, others strike Him on the face; others put on Him a crown of thorns; others give Him great blows. He is pushed; He is thrown down; He is trodden under foot; He is crucified; His heart is pierced. . . . . Oh! if I had known what it is to be a priest, I should very soon have run away to La Trappe."

It is impossible to describe how much he had the salvation of souls at heart. He might be said to be always sighing over the loss of souls. He has often been heard to repeat from the depths of his soul:

"What a pity that souls which have cost the good God so many sufferings should be lost for eternity! Nothing afflicts the Heart of Jesus so much as to see all His sufferings of no avail to so many. . . . . Let us pray, then, for the conversion of sinners; it is the most beautiful and the most useful of all prayers. For the just are on their way to heaven, and the souls in purgatory are sure of getting there. . . . But poor sinners! poor sinners! . . . There are some among them in suspense. One *Pater* and *Ave* would be enough to turn the scale . . . . . How many souls we may convert by our prayers! He who rescues a soul from hell saves that soul and his own too. All devotions are good, but there is none better than this."

"St. Francis of Assisi was once praying in a wood. 'O Lord,' he said, 'have compassion on poor sinners!' and our Lord appeared to him and said, 'Francis, thy will is conformed to Mine. I am ready to grant thee whatever thou mayest ask.'"

"St. Colette asked for the conversion of a thousand sinners; then, reflecting on it, she was alarmed at the great number, and accused herself of rashness. The Blessed Virgin appeared to her, and showed her the quantity of souls she had converted by her novenas. We may offer ourselves as victims during a week or a fortnight for the conversion of sinners. We suffer from cold or heat; we deprive ourselves of looking at some thing, or of going to see some one, which would give us pleasure; we make a novena; we hear Mass every day of the week for this intention, especially in towns where we have the opportunity. But some people would not go a hundred paces to hear Mass. Those who have the happiness of communicating often may make a novena of Communions. By this holy practice we not only contribute to the glory of God, but we also draw down upon ourselves great abundance of graces."

"You have prayed," said M. Vianney to a priest, who complained to him that he could not change the hearts of his parishioners; "you have prayed, you have wept, you have mourned, you have sighed; but have you fasted? have you watched? have you slept on the ground? have you taken the discipline? Till you have come to this, you must not suppose you have done every thing!"

"M. le Curé," his missionary said to him one day, "if the good God were to give you your choice of going directly to heaven, or remaining on earth to labour for the conversion of sinners, what would you do?"

"I think I should remain here."

"Oh! M. le Curé, is it possible? The saints are so happy in heaven! No more temptations; no more miseries!"

He answered, with an angelic smile, "That is true; but the saints *live upon their income!* They have laboured well, for God punishes idleness, and rewards only labour; but they can no longer glorify God, as we can, by sacrifices for the salvation of souls."

"Would you remain on earth till the end of the world?"

"Just the same."

"In that case you would have plenty of time before you. Would you get up so early in the morning?"

"Oh, yes, my friend, at midnight! I am not afraid of trouble. . . . I should be the happiest of priests, if it were not for the thought of appearing before the tribunal of God with my poor Curé's life."

In saying this, he shed abundance of tears.

Chapter VII.

LOVE OF M. VIANNEY FOR THE POOR.

Next to sinners, those who chiefly occupied M. Vianney's thoughts were the poor. He loved them because our Lord loved them, and because he felt that, having to suffer all sorts of privations, pains, and slights here below, they were the more in need of being sought out, honoured, and consoled.

"How lucky it is that the poor come in this way to beg of us! If they did not come, we should have to go and seek them, and we have not always time. Some people give alms that they may be seen, and praised, and admired . . . Some think they do not receive thanks enough. That will not do ! . . . If you give alms for the world's sake, you are right to complain. But if you do it for the good God, what does it matter whether you are thanked or not? We must do all the good we can to every body, but we must look for our recompense from God alone."

"When we give alms, we should think that we are giving to our Lord, and not to the poor. We often think we are relieving a poor person, and we find it is our Lord . . . Look at St. John of God; he used to wash the feet of the poor before he gave them food. One day, as he was leaning over the feet of a poor man, he saw that this poor man's feet were pierced. He raised his head with emotion, and cried, 'It is Thou, then, O Lord!'" (Here M. Vianney burst into tears.) "Our Lord said to him, 'John, I take pleasure in seeing what care thou takest of My poor;' . . . and He disappeared."

"Look at the good St. Gregory, who fed twelve poor men every day at his own table. One day there were thirteen, and he said to his servant, 'There are thirteen poor men.' The servant answered, 'I see only twelve.' The saint observed that this thirteenth changed colour; he was sometimes crimson, and sometimes as white as snow. When the repast was over, the Pope took this poor stranger by the hand, and, leading him aside, asked him, 'Who art thou?'

"'I am an angel'" (here the holy Curé wept again), "'and our Lord sent me to consider closely the care you bestow on His poor. It is I who present to God your prayers and your alms.' After these words, he disappeared. The table at which the angel sat may still be seen in Rome."

"Some people say to the poor who seem to be in good health, 'You are idle; you could work very well; you are young and strong.' But you do not know whether it is not the will of God that this poor person should beg his bread, and thus you run the risk of opposing the will of God."

"Look at the blessed Benedict Labre; every one repulsed him. He was called lazy. The children threw stones at him. This good saint knew that he was doing the will of God; he never answered a word. He once went to his confessor, who said to him, 'My friend, I think you would do better to go into service; you make people offend the good God. The world says it is only laziness that makes you beg.' Benedict Labre answered very humbly, 'Father, it is the will of God that I should beg. Draw the curtain of your confessional, and you will see.' . . . This priest opened it, and saw a light which lighted up all the chapels. He certainly took care not to hinder him in his way of life. . . . . . Well, my children, how do we know that there are not some like him? Therefore we should never repulse the poor. If we cannot give them any thing, we may pray God to inspire others to do so."

"Some will say, 'Oh! he makes a bad use of it.' Let him make what use of it he will, the poor man will be judged by the use he has made of your alms, and you will be judged for the alms that you might have given and did not give."

"We must never despise the poor, because that contempt is reflected back upon God."

Chapter VIII.

HUMILITY OF M. VIANNEY.

Those who did not know the Curé of Ars, and who heard of the wonders worked around him and of the ovations of the multitude, naturally supposed that in this atmosphere of praise and honour, pride would be at least a temptation to him, if not a snare. What a difficulty indeed to remain humble amid the loudest and most striking expressions of public veneration! This idea was alluded to one day in his presence; he raised his eyes to heaven with an expression of profound sadness and almost of despondency, and said, "Ah! if only I were not tempted to despair!"

One day he received a letter full of insults, and soon after, another, expressing nothing but affection and confidence, and calling him a saint. He showed them to his dear daughters of the Providence. "See," said he, "the danger of trusting to human feelings. This morning I should have lost the peace of my soul if I had paid attention to the insults that were addressed to me; and this evening I should have been greatly tempted to pride if I had listened to all those compliments. Oh, how prudent it is not to dwell upon the vain opinions and discourse of men, nor to take any account of them!"

He said also on another occasion, "I received two letters by the same post; one said that I was a great saint, and the other that I was a hypocrite and an impostor. . . . The first added nothing to me, and the second took nothing from me. We are what we are before God, *and nothing more!*" . . . .

Another time he said, "The good God has chosen me to be the instrument of the graces

He bestows on sinners, because I am the most ignorant and the most miserable of priests. If there had been in the diocese a priest more ignorant and more miserable than me, God would have chosen him in preference."

This sentence often recurred in his conversation: "When people speak ill of you, they say what is true ; when they pay you compliments, they are laughing at you. . . . Which is best, that you should be warned, or that you should be misled ? that you should be treated seriously, or in joke?

M. Vianney never spoke of himself of his own accord. If he was questioned he answered modestly and shortly, and turned the conversation. But on such occasions he was ingenious in finding phrases of contempt for himself. He was praising a priest whom he esteemed, and said, in his figurative language, that he had the qualities of the swallow and of the eagle.

"And you, M. le Curé,—what have you?"

"Oh! what have I ? The Curé of Ars is made up of a goose, a turkey, and a crab."

"How good you are," said the holy man to a missionary lately arrived at Ars, "to come to help us!"

"M. le Curé, to say nothing of the pleasure of living with you, we are only doing our duty."

"Oh, no! it is a charity."

"M. le Curé, do not suppose that. There is no charity on our part."

"Oh, yes! You see plainly that all goes well when you are here; but when I am quite alone I am good for nothing. I am like ciphers, which have no value but by the side of other figures. . . . I am too old—I am worth nothing."

"M. le Curé, you are still young in heart and mind."

"Yes, my friend; I may say, like that saint who was asked how old he was, I have not yet lived one day."

To satisfy his desire of lowering and vilifying himself, he continually employed the word *poor*. He spoke of his poor soul, his poor body, his poor misery, his poor sins. He was always ready to publish his faults, and according to himself, his whole life would not have sufficed to weep for them. He was always accusing himself.

The humility of his heart made him shed tears over his weakness and ignorance, and these tears could be dried only by his generous courage, which led him to throw himself with all his failings into the arms of God. He so reproached himself, that one would have thought he had grown old in evil-doing, and that he was the vilest and most wretched of sinners. "How good is God," he often said, "to bear with my immense miseries !"

"God has granted me this great mercy, that He has given me nothing in which I could trust, neither talent, nor science, nor strength, nor virtue. . . . When I reflect upon myself, I can discover nothing but my poor sins. And the good God does not allow me to see them all, or to know myself thoroughly. The sight would drive me to despair. I have no other resource against that temptation to despair but to throw myself at the foot of the tabernacle, like a little dog at its master's feet." . .

The servant of God was one of the few who speak humbly of humility. "M. le Curé, what am I to do to be good?" some one asked him.

"My friend, you must love the good God."

"And what am I to do in order to love God ?"

"Ah ! my friend, humility ! humility ! it is our pride that prevents us from becoming saints. Pride is the chain of the chaplet of all the vices, and humility the chain of the chaplet of all the virtues. Alas ! it is inconceivable how, and of what, such little creatures as we are can be proud ! . . . The devil appeared one day to St. Macarius, armed with a whip, as if to beat him, and said, 'All that thou dost, I do; thou fastest, I never eat; thou watchest, I never sleep. There is only one thing that thou dost, and I cannot do.' 'What is it, then?' 'To humble myself,' answered the devil, and he disappeared. Ah! my friend, there were saints who put the devil to flight by saying, 'How miserable I am!'"

These are some of his thoughts on this subject:

"Humility is like a pair of scales; the more we lower ourselves on one side, the more we rise on the other."

"Those who humble us are our friends, and not those who praise us."

"A saint was asked what was the first virtue? He answered, 'Humility.' And the second? 'Humility.' And the third? 'Humility.'"

"We never understand our poor misery. It makes one shudder to think of it! God gives us only a little glimpse of it."

"If we knew ourselves as He knows us, we could not live; we should die of fear."

"The saints knew themselves better than others, and that is why they were humble. They were covered with confusion when they found that God made use of them to work miracles. St. Martin was a great saint, and thought himself a great sinner. He attributed all the evils that happened in his time to his own sins."

Chapter IX.

THOUGHTS OF M. VIANNEY ON SELF-DENIAL AND SUFFERING.

M. VIANNEY, like all the saints, was convinced that detachment is the one only treasure of the heart; that to sacrifice is not to destroy, but to give life and liberty to the soul, by freeing it from the chains of finite things. Therefore, he always insisted much on death to self, and renouncement of our will.

"Our will," he said, "is the only thing that we have of our own, and can make an offering of to the good God. Therefore, we are assured that a single act of renouncement of the will is more pleasing to Him than a fast of thirty days."

"Every time we can renounce our own will to do that of others, provided it is not against the law of God, we acquire great merits, which are known to God alone. What is it that makes the religious life so meritorious? It is the renouncement of the will at every moment; the continual death to all that has most life in us.

Do you know, I have often thought that the life of a poor servant-girl, who has no will but that of her master, if she knows how to profit by this renouncement, may be as pleasing to God as that of a religious, always following her rule."

"Even in the world, we may every moment find the opportunity of renouncing our will; we may deprive ourselves of a visit that gives us pleasure; we may do a troublesome work of charity; we may go to bed two minutes later, get up two minutes earlier; when two things are to be done, we may choose that one which is the least pleasant."

"I have known some beautiful souls in the world, who had no will of their own, and were quite dead to themselves. That is what the saints do. Look at that good little St. Maurus, who had such power with God, and was so dear to his Superior on account of his simplicity and obedience. The other religious were jealous of him, and the Superior said to them, 'I will show you why I esteem that dear little brother so highly.' He made the tour of the cells; they all had something to finish before they opened their doors; St. Maurus alone, who was copying the Holy Scriptures, instantly left his work to answer the call of St. Benedict."

"It is only the first step that is difficult in this way of abnegation. When once it is entered upon, we go straight forward; and when we have acquired this virtue, we have every thing."

Speaking of the Cross, he said that it was the most learned book that could be read; that those who did not know this book were ignorant, even if they were acquainted with every other; that they alone were wise who loved it, consulted it, fathomed it; that, bitter as it was, nothing was so pleasing as to plunge into the depths of its bitterness; that it was a school where was to be found all knowledge without weariness, and every sweetness without satiety.

"A house founded on the Cross," he said, "will fear neither wind, nor rain, nor storm. Trials show clearly how pleasing a work is to God."

At a time when he was overwhelmed with contradictions, he was on the point of addressing a letter to his Bishop, which would have effectually relieved him from a part of his troubles. The letter was written, but when it was given him to sign, he tore it up, saying, "This is Friday, the day our Lord bore His Cross; I must bear mine. To-day the chalice of humiliation is less bitter."

Chapter X.

HOW M. VIANNEY SPOKE OF THE SAINTS.

M. Vianney spoke often of the saints, and never without tears. His stories of them were so full of life and detail, that one would have thought he had lived in the most intimate intercourse with them. The legends in the lives of the servants of God chiefly attracted him, and he was most delighted with what was most wonderful and contrary to the ordinary course of nature. He differed entirely from those who would limit the power of God, and leave out the supernatural from the lives of the saints, for he had that courage of faith which does not fear to oppose the pride of human reason and to scandalise the impious.

"I think," he said, "that if we had faith we should be masters of the will of God; we should lead it captive, and He would refuse us nothing." Then he had a thousand stories to relate of the divine condescension towards the saints, one more beautiful and marvellous than the other. He spoke of a saint who was burning with desire to adore our Lord in the Sacrament of His love, during the night; he had only to go to a church, and the gates opened of their own accord to let him in.

"Another saint, being in a church, prostrate before a veiled statue of the Most Holy Virgin, was so desirous to see the face of the Mother of God, that the veil which covered the image withdrew of itself, and our Lady appeared to him smiling and beautiful."

"A saint one day met a little shepherd crying bitterly, because one of his sheep was just dead. Touched with compassion, he recalled the poor beast to life."

"There was once a saint who had bought a field, and the man who had sold it to him died soon after; but they pretended afterwards that he had not paid for it, and that the field did not belong to him. He was not at all disturbed, but put all his confidence in God, and answered those who troubled him, 'Give me three days, and I will bring a witness.' He passed that time in praying and fasting, and the third day he went to the place where the man was buried, collected his bones, and said to him, 'Arise, come out of the tomb, and bear witness to the truth.' ... Then those bones returned to human form; the dead man arose and declared before all the bystanders that the field had been duly paid for."

"There was a saint who wanted to build a monastery, but a mountain was in the way. He commanded it to move, and the mountain went back fifty feet."

"Another was asked to command a great rock to change its place. 'Will you be converted if I do it?' said he. 'Yes.' He commanded the rock, and it immediately disappeared in the air."

"See," added the good Curé, weeping, "see how good God is to those who love Him! He works miracles for nothing when one of His friends asks Him. When man has a pure heart, he commands God as if he were His master. St. Francis of Paula heard one day that his parents were to be put to death because a man had been found assassinated in their garden, and they were accused of having killed him. Then he said, 'O Lord, let me be near them to-morrow!' In the night an angel transported him four hundred leagues, to the country where they were. The next day he said before every body, 'Bring hither the man who has been killed.' They brought him; and he said, 'I command thee, in the name of God, to declare whether it was my parents that killed thee.' And the man arose, and exclaimed before them all, 'No, it was not thy parents.' Then the saint said again to our Lord, 'Let me be taken back to my monastery;' and during the night the angel took him away again. He travelled in this way eight hundred leagues. The good God can refuse nothing to a pure heart."

"St. Vincent Ferrer worked so many miracles that his Superior, fearing they might prove a snare to his humility, forbade him to exercise, without permission, the power he had received from God. One day he was in adoration before our Lord, and a workman who was repairing the church fell from the top of a scaffold. The good saint cried out to him, 'Stop ! stop ! I have not the power to raise you to life again.' Then he went in haste to get the permission he required from his Superior, who was very much surprised, and could not understand the matter; being sure that, at any rate, the permission would come too late. What was his astonishment when, following St. Vincent to the place of the accident, he saw suspended in the air the unfortunate mason whom he expected to find lying on the ground ! 'Come,' said he to the saint, 'do whatever you wish. Indeed, there is no way of preventing you.' "

These stories were the more attractive from the tender simplicity with which he related them. Nothing could be more touching and beautiful than the frequent tears, the angelic smiles, the innocent joyfulness that were combined in him, with thoughts so lofty, with habits of life so austere, with sacrifices so painful, and an apostolate so laborious. In an age when simplicity has almost disappeared from among men, no Christian can see without emotion and envy how this holy priest fulfilled the words of our Lord, that we should become like little children.

His cheerfulness and benevolence were never diminished by labour and suffering, but seemed, on the contrary, to increase amid the infirmities of old age. That gloomy period was replaced in him by a freshness of feeling and imagination which overcame the chills of age, like the eternal youth of the blessed. He never knew that sadness which makes the decline of life silent and melancholy, casting a shadow over the soul.

The conversations we had with him two months before his death have often recalled to our mind these words: "The last thoughts of a heart filled with the love of God are like the last rays of the sun, more intense and more brilliant on the point of disappearing."

PART IV.

SEVENTEEN EXHORTATIONS OF THE CURÉ OF ARS.

I.

The happiness of man on earth, my children, is to be very good; those who are very good bless the good God, they love Him, they glorify Him, and do all their works with joy and love, because they know that we are in this world for no other end than to serve and love the good God.

Look at bad Christians; they do every thing with trouble and disgust; and why, my children? because they do not love the good God, because their soul is not pure, and their hopes are no longer in heaven, but on earth. Their heart is an impure source which poisons all their actions, and prevents them from rising to God; so they come to die without having thought of death, destitute of good works for heaven, and loaded with crimes for hell: this is the way they are lost for ever, my children. People say it is too much trouble to save one's soul; but, my children, is it not trouble to acquire glory or fortune? Do you stay in bed when you have to go and plough, or mow, or reap? No. Well, then, why should you be more idle when you have to lay up an immense fortune which will never perish—when you have to strive for eternal glory? . . .

See, my children, if we really wish to be saved, we must determine, once for all, to labour in earnest for our salvation; our soul is like a garden in which the weeds are ever ready to choke the good plants and flowers that have been sown in it. If the gardener who has charge of this garden neglects it, if he is not continually using the spade and the hoe, the flowers and plants will soon disappear. Thus, my children, do the virtues with which God has been pleased to adorn our soul disappear under our vices, if we neglect to cultivate them. As a vigilant gardener labours from morning till night to destroy the weeds in his garden, and to ornament it with flowers, so let us labour every day to extirpate the vices of our soul and to adorn it with virtues. See, my children, a gardener never lets the weeds take root, because he knows that then he would never be able to destroy them. Neither let us allow our vices to take root, or we shall not be able to conquer them.

One day, an anchorite being in a forest with a companion, showed him four cypresses to be pulled up one after the other ; the young man, who did not very well know why he told him to do this, took hold of the first tree, which was quite small, and pulled it up with one hand without any trouble; the second, which was a little bigger and had some roots, made him pull harder, but yet he pulled it up with one hand ; the third, being still bigger, offered so much resistance, that he was obliged to take both hands and to use all his strength; the fourth, which was grown into a tree, had such deep roots, that he exhausted himself in vain efforts. The saint then said to him, " With a little vigilance and mortification, we succeed in repressing our passions, and we triumph over them when they are only springing up ; but when they have taken deep root, nothing is more difficult; the thing is even impossible without a miracle."

Let us not reckon on a miracle of Providence, my children ; let us not put off till the end of our life the care that we ought daily to take of our soul ; let us labour while it is yet time,— later it will no longer be within our power; let us lay our hands to the work; let us watch over ourselves; above all, let us pray to the good God,—with His assistance we shall always have power over our passions. Man sins, my children; but if he has not in this first moment lost the faith, he runs, he hastens, he flies, to seek a remedy for his ill; he cannot soon enough find the tribunal of penance, where he can recover his happiness. That is the way we should conduct ourselves if we were good Christians. Yes, my children, we could not remain one moment under the empire of the devil; we should be ashamed of being his slaves. A good Christian watches continually, sword in hand, and the devil can do nothing against him, for he resists him like a warrior in full armour; he does not fear him, because he has rejected from his heart all that is impure. Bad Christians are idle and lazy, and stand hanging their heads; and you see how they give way at the first assault; the devil does what he pleases with them; he presents pleasure to them, he makes them taste pleasure, and then, to drown the cries of their conscience, he whispers to them in a gentle voice, " Thou wilt sin no more."

And when the occasion presents itself, they fall again, and more easily than the first time. If they go to confession he makes them ashamed, they speak only in half-words, they lower their voice, they explain away their sins, and, what is more miserable, they perhaps conceal some. The good Christian, on the contrary, groans and weeps over his sins, and reaches the tribunal of penance half justified.

II.

ON DEATH.

A DAY will come, perhaps it is not far off, when we must bid adieu to life, adieu to the world, adieu to our relations, adieu to our friends. When shall we return, my children? Never. We appear upon this earth, we disappear, and we return no more; our poor body, that we take such care of, goes away into dust, and our soul, all trembling, goes to appear before the good God.

When we quit this world, where we shall appear no more, when our last breath of life escapes, and we say our last adieu, we shall wish to have passed our life in solitude, in the depths of a desert, far from the world and its pleasures.

We have these examples of repentance before our eyes every day, my children, and we remain always the same. We pass our life gaily, without ever troubling ourselves about eternity. By our indifference to the service of the good God, one would think we were never going to die.

See, my children, some people pass their whole life without thinking of death. It comes, and behold! they have nothing; faith, hope, love, all are already dead within them.

When death shall come upon us, of what use will three-quarters of our life have been to us? With what are we occupied the greatest part of our time? Are we thinking of the good God, of our salvation, of our soul?

O my children! what folly is the world! we come into it, we go out of it, without knowing why.

The good God places us in it to serve Him, to try if we will love Him and be faithful to His law; and after this short moment of trial, He promises us a recompense. Is it not just that He should reward the faithful servant and punish the wicked one?

Should the Trappist, who has passed his life in lamenting and weeping over his sins, be treated the same as the bad Christian, who has lived in abundance in the midst of all the enjoyments of life? No; certainly not. We are on earth not to enjoy its pleasures, but to labour for our salvation.

Let us prepare ourselves for death; we have not a minute to lose: it will come upon us at the moment when we least expect it; it will take us by surprise.

Look at the saints, my children, who were pure; they were always trembling, they pined away with fear; and we, who so often offend the good God,—we have no fears. Life is given us that we may learn to die well, and we never think of it. We occupy ourselves with every thing else. The idea of it often occurs to us, and we always reject it; we put it off to the last moment. O my children! this last moment, how much it is to be feared!

Yet the good God does not wish us to despair; He shows us the good thief, touched with repentance, dying near Him on a cross; but he is the only one; and then see, he dies near the good God. Can we hope to be near Him at our last moment—we who have been far from Him all our life? ... What have we done to deserve that favour? ... A great deal of evil, and no good.

There was once a good Trappist Father, who was trembling all over at perceiving the approach of death. Some one said to him, "Father, of what then are you afraid?" "Of the judgment of God," he said. "Ah! if you dread the judgment—you who have done so much penance, you who love God so much, who have been so long preparing for death—what will become of me?"

See, my children, to die well, we must live well; to live well, we must seriously examine ourselves: every evening think over what we have done during the day; at the end of each week review what we have done during the week; at the end of each month review what we have done during the month; at the end of the year, what we have done during the year. By this means, my children, we cannot fail to correct ourselves, and to become fervent Christians in a short time. Then, when death comes, we are quite ready, we are happy to go to Heaven.

III.

ON THE LAST JUDGMENT.

Our Catechism tells us, my children, that all men will undergo a particular judgment on the day of their death. No sooner shall we have breathed our last sigh than our soul, without leaving the place where it has expired, will be presented before the tribunal of God. Wherever we may die, God is there to exercise His justice.

The good God, my children, has measured out our years, and of those years that He has resolved to leave us on this earth, He has marked out one which shall be our last; one day which we shall not see succeeded by other days; one hour after which there will be for us no more time... What distance is there between that moment and this?—the space of an instant.

Life, my children, is a smoke, a light vapour; it disappears more quickly than a bird that darts through the air, or a ship that sails on the sea, and leaves no trace of its course!

When shall we die? Alas! will it be in a year, in a month?—perhaps to-morrow, perhaps to-day! May not that happen to us which happens to so many others?

It may be that at a moment when you are thinking of nothing but amusing yourself, you may be summoned to the judgment of God, like the impious Baltassar. What will then be the astonishment of that soul entering on its eternity? Surprised, bewildered, separated thenceforth from its relations and friends, and, as it were, surrounded with Divine light, it will find in its Creator no longer a merciful Father, but an inflexible Judge.

Imagine to yourselves, my children, a soul at its departure from this life. It is going to appear before the tribunal of its Judge, alone with God; there is heaven on one side, hell on the other. What object presents itself before it?... The picture of its whole life!.... All its thoughts, all its words, all its actions, are examined.

This examination will be terrible, my children, because nothing is hidden from God; His infinite science knows our most inmost thoughts; it penetrates to the bottom of our hearts, and lays open their innermost folds.

In vain sinners avoid the light of day that they may sin more freely: they spare themselves a little shame in the eyes of men, but it will be of no advantage to them at the day of judgment; God will make light the darkness under cover of which they thought to sin with impunity. The Holy Ghost, my children, says that we shall be examined on our words, our thoughts, our actions; we shall be examined even on the good we ought to have done, and have not done, on the sins of others of which we have been the cause. Alas! so many thoughts to which we abandon ourselves—to which the mind gives itself up: how many in one day! in a week! in a month! in a year! . . . How many in the whole course of our life! Not one of this infinite number will escape the knowledge of our Judge.

The proud man must give an account of all his thoughts of presumption, of vanity, of ambition; the impure of all his evil thoughts, and of the criminal desires with which he has fed his imagination. Those young people who are incessantly occupied with their dress, who are seeking to please, to distinguish themselves, to attract attention and praise, and who dare not make themselves known in the tribunal of penance, will they be able still to hide themselves at the day of the judgment of God? No, no! . . . They will appear there such as they have been during their life, before Him who makes known all that is most secret in the heart of man.

We shall give an account, my children, of our oaths, of our imprecations, of our curses. God hears our slanders, our calumnies, our free conversations, our worldly and licentious songs; He hears also the discourse of the impious.

This is not all, my children; God will also examine our actions. He will bring to light all our unfaithfulness in His service, our forgetfulness of His commandments, our transgression of His law, the profanation of His churches, the attachment to the world, the ill-regulated love of pleasure and of the perishable goods of earth. All, my children, will be unveiled; those thefts, that injustice, that usury, that intemperance, that anger, those disputes, that tyranny, that revenge, those criminal liberties, those abominations that cannot be named without blushes. . . .

IV.

ON SIN.

Sin is a thought, a word, an action, contrary to the law of God.

By sin, my children, we rebel against the good God, we despise His justice, we tread under foot His blessings.

From being children of God, we become the executioner and assassin of our soul, the offspring of hell, the horror of heaven, the murderer of Jesus Christ, the capital enemy of the good God. . . .

O my children! if we thought of this, if we reflected on the injury which sin offers to the good God, we should hold it in abhorrence, we should be unable to commit it; but we never think of it, we like to live at our ease, we slumber in sin.

If the good God sends us remorse, we quickly stifle it, by thinking that we have done no harm to any body, that God is good, and that He did not place us on the earth to make us suffer.

Indeed, my children, the good God did not place us on the earth to suffer and endure, but to work out our salvation. See; He wills that we should work to-day and to-morrow ; and after that, an eternity of joy, of happiness, awaits us in heaven. . . .

O my children! how ungrateful we are! The good God calls us to Himself; He wishes to make us happy for ever, and we are deaf to His word, we will not share His happiness; He enjoins us to love Him, and we give our heart to the devil. . . .

The good God commands all nature as its Master; He makes the winds and the storms obey Him; the angels tremble at His adorable will; man alone dares to resist Him.

See; God forbids us that action, that criminal pleasure, that revenge, that injustice; no matter, we are bent upon satisfying ourselves; we had rather renounce the happiness of heaven, than deprive ourselves of a moment's pleasure, or give up a sinful habit, or change our life. What are we, then, that we dare thus to resist God? Dust and ashes, which He could annihilate with a single look. . . .

By sin, my children, we despise the good God. . . . We renew His Death and Passion; we do as much evil as all the Jews together did, in fastening Him to the Cross. Therefore, my children, if we were to ask those who work without necessity on Sunday: " What are you doing there?" and they were to answer truly, they would say, " We are crucifying the good God."

Ask the idle, the gluttonous, the immodest,

what they do every day. If they answer you according to what they are really doing, they will say, " We are crucifying the good God."

O my children! it is very ungrateful to offend a God who has never done us any harm; but is it not the height of ingratitude to offend a God who has done us nothing but good? . . . .

It is He who created us, who watches over us. He holds us in His hands, like a handful of hair; if He chose, He could cast us into the nothingness out of which he took us. He has given us His Son, to redeem us from the slavery of the devil; He Himself gave Him up to death, that He might restore us to life; He has adopted us as His children, and ceases not to lavish His graces upon us. Notwithstanding all this, what use do we make of our mind, of our memory, of our health, of those limbs which he gave us to serve Him with? We employ them perhaps in committing crimes. . . .

The good God, my children, has given us eyes to enlighten us, to see heaven, and we use them to look at criminal and dangerous objects; He has given us a tongue to praise Him, and to express our thoughts, and we make it an instrument of iniquity,—we swear, we blaspheme, we speak ill of our neighbour, we slander him; we abuse the supernatural graces, we stifle the salutary remorse, by which God would convert us; . . . we reject the inspirations of our good guardian angel.

We despise good thoughts, we neglect prayer and the Sacraments. What account do we make even of the Word of God? . . . Do we not listen to it with disgust? How miserable we are! How much we are to be pitied! We employ in losing our souls the time that the good God has given us to save them in.

We make war upon Him with the means He has given us to serve Him; we turn His own gifts against Him! . . .

Let us cast our eyes, my children, upon Jesus fastened to the Cross, and let us say to ourselves, "This is what it has cost my Saviour to repair the injury my sins have done to God." . . .

A God coming down to the earth to be the victim of our sins! A God suffering, a God dying, a God enduring every torment, because He has put on the semblance of sin, and has chosen to bear the weight of our iniquities! . . .

Ah! my children, at the sight of that Cross, let us conceive once for all the malice of sin, and the abhorrence in which we should hold it. . . .

Let us enter into ourselves, and see what we ought to do to repair our past sins; let us implore the clemency of the good God, and let us all together say to Him, from the bottom of our heart, " O Lord, who art here crucified for us, have mercy upon us! . . . Thou comest down from heaven to cure souls of sin; cure us, we beseech Thee; cause our souls to be purified by approaching the tribunal of penance; yes, O God! make us look upon sin as the greatest of all evils, and by our zeal in avoiding it, and in repairing those we have had the misfortune to commit, let us one day attain to the happiness of the saints."

V.

ON TEMPTATIONS.

We are all inclined to sin, my children; we are idle, greedy, sensual, given to the pleasures of the flesh.

We want to know every thing, to learn every thing, to see every thing; we must watch over our mind, over our heart, and over our senses, for these are the gates by which the devil penetrates. See, he prowls round us incessantly; his only occupation in this world is to seek companions for himself. All our life he will lay snares for us, he will try to make us yield to temptations; we must, on our side, do all we can to defeat and resist him.

We can do nothing by ourselves, my children; but we can do every thing with the help of the good God ; let us pray Him to deliver us from this enemy of our salvation, or to give us strength to fight against him. With the Name of Jesus we shall overthrow the demons ; we shall put them to flight. With this Name, if they sometimes dare to attack us, our battles will be victories, and our victories will be crowns for heaven, all brilliant with precious stones.

See, my children, the good God refuses nothing to those who pray to Him from the bottom of their heart. St. Teresa, being one day in prayer, and desiring to see the good God, Jesus Christ showed to the eyes of her soul His divine Hands ; then, another day, when she was again in prayer, He showed her His Face. Lastly, some days after, He showed her the whole of His Sacred Humanity.

The good God who granted the desire of St. Teresa will also grant our prayers. If we ask of Him the grace to resist temptations, He will grant it to us ; for He wishes to save us all, He shed His Blood for us all, He died for us all, He is waiting for us all in heaven ; we are two or three hundred here : shall we all be saved, shall we all go to heaven ? Alas ! my children, we know nothing about it ; but I tremble when I see so many souls lost in these days.

See, they fall into hell as the leaves fall from the trees at the approach of winter. We shall fall like the rest, my children, if we do not avoid temptations; if, when we cannot avoid them, we do not fight generously, with the help of the good God,—if we do not invoke His Name during the strife, like St. Antony in the desert.

This saint having retired into an old sepulchre, the devil came to attack him; he tried at first to terrify him with a horrible noise; he even beat him so cruelly, that he left him half dead and covered with wounds. "Well," said St. Antony, "here I am, ready to fight again; no, thou shalt not be able to separate me from Jesus Christ, my Lord and my God." The spirits of darkness redoubled their efforts, and uttered frightful cries. St. Antony remained unmoved, because he put all his confidence in God. After the example of this saint, my children, let us be always ready for the combat; let us put our confidence in God; let us fast and pray; and the devil will not be able to separate us from Jesus Christ, either in this world or the next.

VI.

ON PRIDE.

Pride is an untrue opinion of ourselves, an untrue idea of what we are not.

The proud man is always disparaging himself, that people may praise him the more. The more the proud man lowers himself, the more he seeks to raise his miserable nothingness. He relates what he has done, and what he has not done; he feeds his imagination with what has been said in praise of him, and seeks by all possible means for more; he is never satisfied with praise. See, my children, if you only show some little displeasure against a man given up to self-love, he gets angry, and accuses you of ignorance or injustice towards him. . . .

My children, we are in reality only what we are in the eyes of God, and nothing more. Is it not quite clear and evident that we are nothing, that we can do nothing, that we are very miserable? Can we lose sight of our sins, and cease to humble ourselves?

If we were to consider well what we are, humility would be easy to us, and the demon of pride would no longer have any room in our heart. See, *our days are like grass,*—like the grass which now flourishes in the meadows, and will presently be withered; like an ear of corn which is fresh only for a moment, and is parched by the sun. In fact, my children, to-day we are full of life, full of health; and to-morrow, death will perhaps come to reap us and mow us down, as you reap your corn and mow your meadows. . . . Whatever appears vigorous, whatever shines, whatever is beautiful, is of short duration. . . . The glory of this world, youth, honours, riches, all pass away quickly, as quickly as the flower of grass, as the flower of the field. . . . Let us reflect that so we shall one day be reduced to dust; . . . that we shall be thrown into the fire like dry grass, if we do not fear the good God.

Good Christians know this very well, my children; therefore they do not occupy themselves with their body; they despise the affairs of this world; they consider only their soul and how to unite it to God.

Can we be proud in the face of the examples of lowliness, of humiliations, that our Lord has given us, and is still giving us every day? Jesus Christ came upon earth, became incarnate, was born poor, lived in poverty, died on a gibbet, between two thieves. . . . He instituted an admirable Sacrament, in which He communicates Himself to us under the Eucharistic veil; and in this Sacrament He undergoes the most extraordinary humiliations. Residing continually in our tabernacles, He is deserted, misunderstood by ungrateful men; and yet He continues to love us, to serve us in the Sacrament of the Altar. . . .

O my children! what an example of humiliation does the good Jesus give us! . . .

Behold Him on the Cross to which our sins have fastened Him; behold Him: He calls us, and says to us, " Come to Me, and learn of Me, because I am meek and humble of heart." . . .

How well the saints understood this invitation, my children! Therefore, they all sought humiliations and sufferings. After their example, then, let us not be afraid of being humbled and despised.

St. John of God, at the beginning of his conversion, counterfeited madness, ran about the streets, and was followed by the populace, who threw stones at him: he always came in covered with mud and with blood. He was shut up as a madman; the most violent remedies were employed to cure him of his pretended illness; and he bore it all in the spirit of penance, and in expiation of his past sins.

The good God, my children, does not require of us extraordinary things. He wills that we should be gentle, humble, and modest; then we shall always be pleasing to Him; we shall be like little children; and He will grant us the grace to come to Him and to enjoy the happiness of the saints.

VII.

ON AVARICE.

Our catechism teaches us that *avarice is an inordinate love of the goods of this world.*

Yes, my children, it is an ill-regulated love, a fatal love, which makes us forget the good God, prayer, the Sacraments, that we may love the goods of this world—gold and silver and lands. The avaricious man is like a pig, which seeks its food in the mud, without caring where it comes from. Stooping towards the earth, he thinks of nothing but the earth; he no longer looks towards heaven, his happiness is no longer there. The avaricious man does no good till after his death. See how greedily he gathers up wealth, how anxiously he keeps it, how afflicted he is if he loses it. In the midst of riches, he does not enjoy them; he is, as it were, plunged in a river, and is dying of thirst; lying on a heap of corn, he is dying of hunger; he has every thing, my children, and dares not touch any thing; his gold is a sacred thing to him, he makes it his divinity, he adores it. . . .

O my children! how many there are in these days who are idolaters! how many there are who think more of making a fortune than of serving the good God! They steal, they defraud, they go to law with their neighbour; they do not even respect the laws of God. They work on Sundays and holidays: nothing comes amiss to their greedy and rapacious hands. . .

Good Christians, my children, do not think of their body, which must end in corruption; they think only of their soul, which is immortal. While they are on the earth, they occupy themselves with their soul alone. So you see how assiduous they are at the Offices of the Church, with what fervour they pray before the good God, how they sanctify the Sunday, how recollected they are at holy Mass, how happy they are! The days, the months, the years are nothing to them; they pass them in loving the good God, with their eyes fixed on their eternity. . . .

Seeing us so indifferent to our salvation, and so occupied in gathering up a little mud, would not any one say that we were never to die?

Indeed, my children, we are like people who, during the summer, should make an ample provision of gourds, of melons, for a long journey; after the winter, what would remain of it?—nothing.

In the same way, my children, what remains to the avaricious man of all his wealth when death comes upon him unawares? A poor covering, a few planks, and the despair of not being able to carry his gold away with him. Misers generally die in this sort of despair, and pay eternally to the devil for their insatiable thirst of riches.

Misers, my children, are sometimes punished even in this world.

Once St. Hilarion, followed by a great number of his disciples, going to visit the monasteries under his rule, came to the abode of an avaricious solitary. On their approach, they found watchers in all parts of the vineyard, who threw stones and clods of earth at them to prevent their touching the grapes. This miser was well punished, for he gathered that year much fewer grapes than usual, and his wine turned into vinegar.

Another solitary, named Sabbas, begged him, on the contrary, to come into his vineyard and eat the fruit. St. Hilarion blessed it, and sent into it his religious, to the number of three thousand, who all satisfied their hunger ; and twenty days after, the vineyard yielded three hundred measures of wine, instead of the usual quantity of ten.

Let us follow the example of Sabbas, and be disinterested ; the good God will bless us, and after having blessed us in this world, He will also reward us in the other.

VIII.

ON LUXURY.

Luxury is the love of the pleasures that are contrary to purity.

No sins, my children, ruin and destroy a soul so quickly as this shameful sin ; it snatches us out of the hands of the good God, and hurls us like a stone into an abyss of mire and corruption. Once plunged in this mire, we cannot get out, we make a deeper hole in it every day, we sink lower and lower. Then we lose the faith, we laugh at the truths of religion, we no longer see heaven, we do not fear hell. O my children! how much are they to be pitied who give way to this passion! how wretched they are! Their soul, which was so beautiful, which attracted the eyes of the good God, over which He leant as one leans over a perfumed rose, has become like a rotten carcass, of which the pestilential odour rises even to His throne. . .

See, my children ; Jesus Christ endured patiently, among His Apostles, men who were proud, ambitious, greedy,—even one who betrayed Him ; but He could not bear the least stain of impurity in any of them ; it is of all vices that which He has most in abhorrence: "My Spirit does not dwell in you," the Lord says, "if you are nothing but flesh and corruption."

God gives up the impure, then, to all the wicked inclinations of his heart. He lets him wallow, like the vile swine, in the mire, and does not even let him smell its offensive exhalations. . . .

The immodest man is odious to every one, and is not aware of it. God has set the mark of ignominy on his forehead, and he is not ashamed; he has a face of brass and a heart of bronze; it is in vain you talk to him of honour, of virtue: he is full of nothing but arrogance and pride. The eternal truths, death, judgment, paradise, hell,—nothing terrifies him, nothing can move him.

So, my children, of all sins that of impurity is the most difficult to eradicate. Other sins forge for us chains of iron, but this one makes them of bull's-hide, which can be neither broken nor rent; it is a fire, a furnace, which consumes even to the most advanced old age.

See those two infamous old men who attempted the purity of the chaste Susannah; they had kept the fire of their youth even till they were decrepit. When the body is worn out with debauchery, when they can no longer satisfy their passions, they supply the place of it, oh, shame! by infamous desires and memories.

With one foot in the grave, they still speak

the language of passion, till their last breath; they die as they have lived, impenitent; for what penance can be done by the impure, what sacrifice can he impose on himself at his death, who during his life has always given way to his passions? Can one at the last moment expect a good confession, a good communion, from him who has concealed one of these shameful sins, perhaps, from his earliest youth—who has heaped sacrilege on sacrilege? Will the tongue, which has been silent up to this day, be unloosed at the last moment? No, no, my children; God has abandoned him; many sheets of lead already weigh upon him; he will add another, and it will be the last. . . .

IX.

ON ENVY.

Envy is a sadness which we feel, on account of the good that happens to our neighbour.

Envy, my children, follows pride; whoever is envious is proud. See, envy comes to us from hell; the devils having sinned through pride, sinned also through envy, envying our glory, our happiness.

Why do we envy the happiness and the

goods of others? Because we are proud; we should like to be the sole possessors of talents, riches, of the esteem and love of all the world. We hate our equals, because they are our equals; our inferiors, from the fear that they may equal us; our superiors, because they are above us.

In the same way, my children, that the devil after his fall felt, and still feels, extreme anger at seeing us the heirs of the glory of the good God, so the envious man feels sadness at seeing the spiritual and temporal prosperity of his neighbour.

We walk, my children, in the footsteps of the devil; like him, we are vexed at good, and rejoice at evil. If our neighbour loses any thing, if his affairs go wrong, if he is humbled, if he is unfortunate, we are joyful, . . . we triumph! The devil, too, he is full of joy and triumph when we fall, when he can make us fall as low as himself. What does he gain by it? . . . . Nothing.

Shall we be richer, because our neighbour is poorer? Shall we be greater, because he is less? Shall we be happier, because he is more unhappy? . . . O my children! how much we are to be pitied for being like this!

St. Cyprian said that other evils had limits, but that envy had none. In fact, my children, the envious man invents all sorts of wickedness; he has recourse to evil speaking, to calumny, to cunning, in order to blacken his neighbour; he repeats what he knows, and what he does not know he invents, he exaggerates. . . .

Through the envy of the devil, death entered into the world; and also through envy we kill our neighbour; by dint of malice, of falsehood, we make him lose his reputation, his place. . . .

Good Christians, my children, do not do so; they envy no one; they love their neighbour; they rejoice at the good that happens to him, and they weep with him if any misfortune comes upon him. How happy should we be if we were good Christians! . . . Ah! my children, let us, then, be good Christians, and we shall no more envy the good fortune of our neighbour; we shall never speak evil of him; we shall enjoy a sweet peace; our soul will be calm, we shall find paradise on earth.

X.

ON GLUTTONY.

Gluttony is an inordinate love of eating and drinking.

We are gluttonous, my children, when we take food in excess, more than is required for the support of our poor body; when we drink beyond what is necessary, so as even to lose our senses and our reason. . . . Oh, how shameful is this vice! how it degrades us! See, it puts us below the brutes: the animals never drink more than to satisfy their thirst; they content themselves with eating enough; and we, when we have satisfied our appetite, when our body can bear no more, we still have recourse to all sorts of little delicacies; we take wine and liquors to repletion!

Is it not pitiful? We can no longer keep upon our legs; we fall, we roll into the ditch and into the mud, we become the laughing-stock of every one, even the sport of little children. . . .

If death were to surprise us in this state, my children, we should not have time to recollect ourselves; we should fall in that state into the hands of the good God. What a misfortune, my children! How would our soul be surprised! How it would be astonished! We should shudder with horror at seeing the lost who are in hell. . . .

Do not let us be led by our appetite; we shall ruin our health, we shall lose our soul. . . . See, my children, intemperance and debauchery are the support of doctors; that lets them live, and gives them a great deal of practice. . . .

We hear every day, such a one was drunk, and falling down he broke his leg; another, passing a river on a plank, fell into the water and was drowned. . . .

Intemperance and drunkenness are the companions of the wicked rich man. . . .

A moment of pleasure in this world will cost us very dear in the other. There they will be tormented by a raging hunger and a devouring thirst; they will not even have a drop of water to refresh themselves; their tongue and their body will be consumed by the flames for a whole eternity! . . .

O my children! we do not think about it; and yet that will not fail to happen to some amongst us, perhaps even before the end of the year! . . .

St. Paul said, that those who give themselves to excess in eating and drinking shall not possess the kingdom of God. Let us reflect on these words! . . .

Look at the saints: they passed their life in penance, and we would pass ours in the midst of enjoyments and pleasures.

St. Elizabeth, Queen of Portugal, fasted all Advent, and also from St. John Baptist's day to the Assumption. Soon after, she began another

Lent, which lasted till the Feast of St. Michael. She lived upon bread and water only, on Fridays and Saturdays, and on the vigils of the feasts of the Blessed Virgin and of the Apostles.

They say that St. Bernard drank oil for wine. St. Isidore never ate without shedding tears! . . .

If we were good Christians, we should do as the saints have done.

We should gain a great deal for heaven at our meals; we should deprive ourselves of many little things, which, without being hurtful to our body, would be very pleasing to the good God; but we choose rather to satisfy our taste than to please God; we drown, we stifle our soul in wine and food.

My children, God will not say to us at the day of judgment, "Give Me an account of thy body;" but, "Give Me an account of thy soul; what hast thou done with it?" . . . What shall we answer Him? Do we take as much care of our soul as of our body?

O my children! let us no longer live for the pleasure of eating; let us live as the saints have done; let us mortify ourselves as they were mortified. The saints never indulged themselves in the pleasures of good cheer. *Their pleasure was to feed on Jesus Christ!* Let us follow their footsteps on this earth, and we shall gain the crown which they have in heaven.

XI.

ON ANGER.

Anger is an emotion of the soul, which leads us violently to repel whatever hurts or displeases us.

This emotion, my children, comes from the devil; it shows that we are in his hands; that he is the master of our heart; that he holds all the strings of it, and makes us dance as he pleases. See, a person who puts himself in a passion is like a puppet; he knows neither what he says, nor what he does; the devil guides him entirely. He strikes right and left; his hair stands up like the bristles of a hedgehog; his eyes start out of his head,—he is a scorpion, a furious lion...

Why do we, my children, put ourselves into such a state? Is it not pitiable? It is, mind, because we do not love the good God. Our heart is given up to the demon of pride, who is angry when he thinks himself despised; to the demon of avarice, who is irritated when he suffers any loss; to the demon of luxury, who is indignant when his pleasures are interfered with. . . .

How unhappy we are, my children, thus to be the sport of demons! They do whatever they please with us; they suggest to us evil-speaking, calumny, hatred, vengeance; they even drive us so far as to put our neighbour to death. See, Cain killed his brother Abel out of jealousy; Saul wished to take away the life of David; Theodosius caused the massacre of the inhabitants of Thessalonica, to revenge a personal affront. . . .

If we do not put our neighbour to death, we are angry with him, we curse him, we give him to the devil, we wish for his death, we wish for our own. In our fury, we blaspheme the holy Name of God; we accuse His Providence. . . What fury, what impiety! . . . And what is more deplorable, my children, we are carried to these excesses for a trifle, for a word, for the least injustice! Where is our faith? where is our reason? . . . We say in excuse that it is anger that makes us swear; but one sin cannot excuse another sin. The good God equally condemns anger and the excesses that are its consequences. . . . How we sadden our guardian angel! He is always there at our side, to send us good thoughts, and he sees us do nothing but evil . . . If we did like St. Remigius, we should never be angry. See, this saint, being questioned by a Father of the desert how he managed to be always in an even temper, replied, " I often consider that my guardian angel is always by my side, who assists me in all my needs, who tells me what I ought to do and what I ought to say, and who writes down, after each of my actions, the way in which I have done it."

Philip II., King of Spain, having passed several hours of the night in writing a long letter to the Pope, gave it to his secretary to fold up and seal. He, being half asleep, made a mistake; when he meant to put sand on the letter, he took the ink-bottle and covered all the paper with ink. While he was ashamed and inconsolable, the king said, quite calmly, " No very great harm is done; there is another sheet of paper;" and he took it, and employed the rest of the night in writing a second letter, without showing the least displeasure with his secretary. . . .

XII.

ON SLOTH.

WHAT is sloth?
Sloth is a kind of cowardice and disgust,

dren, because nothing is hidden from God; His infinite science knows our most inmost thoughts; it penetrates to the bottom of our hearts, and lays open their innermost folds.

In vain sinners avoid the light of day that they may sin more freely : they spare themselves a little shame in the eyes of men, but it will be of no advantage to them at the day of judgment; God will make light the darkness under cover of which they thought to sin with impunity. The Holy Ghost, my children, says that we shall be examined on our words, our thoughts, our actions ; we shall be examined even on the good we ought to have done, and have not done, on the sins of others of which we have been the cause. Alas! so many thoughts to which we abandon ourselves—to which the mind gives itself up: how many in one day! in a week! in a month! in a year! . . . How many in the whole course of our life! Not one of this infinite number will escape the knowledge of our Judge.

The proud man must give an account of all his thoughts of presumption, of vanity, of ambition; the impure of all his evil thoughts, and of the criminal desires with which he has fed his imagination. Those young people who are incessantly occupied with their dress, who are seeking to please, to distinguish themselves, to attract attention and praise, and we can not make themselves known at the day of penance will they be able ex... selves at the day of the judgment... no!... They n... ... ... have been during their ... ... makes known all that is in the ... ... of man.

We shall give an account in ... ... oaths, of our impressions ... ... hears our slander, our ... ... versations, our words, and ... ... He hears also the ... ...

This is not all, my children ... ... examine our actions. He ... ... our unfaithfulness to His ... ... fulness of His commandments, the ... ... of His law, the profanation of His ... ... attachment to the world, the ... ... of pleasure and of the perishable goods of earth. All, my children, will be ... those thefts, that injustice, that ... ... temperance, that anger, those ... ... tyranny, that revenge, those criminal ... those abominations that cannot be named without blushes. . . .

which makes us neglect and omit our duties, rather than do violence to ourselves.

Alas! my children, how many slothful people there are on this earth; how many are cowardly, how many are indolent in the service of the good God! We neglect, we omit our duties of piety, just as easily as we should take a glass of wine. We will not do violence to ourselves; we will not put ourselves to any inconvenience. Every thing wearies, every thing disgusts the slothful man. Prayer, the holy Sacrifice of the Mass, which do so much good to pious souls, are a torture to him. He is weary and dissatisfied in church, at the foot of the altar, in the presence of the good God. At first he feels only dislike and indifference towards every thing that is commanded by religion. Soon after, you can no longer speak to him either of confession or communion; he has no time to think of those things.

O my children! how miserable we are in losing, in this way, the time that we might so usefully employ in gaining heaven, in preparing ourselves for eternity!

How many moments are lost in doing nothing, or in doing wrong, in listening to the suggestions of the devil, in obeying him! Does not that make us tremble? If one of the lost had only a day or an hour to spend for his salvation, to what profit would he turn it! What haste he would make to save his soul, to reconcile himself with the good God!

And we, my children, who have days and years to think of our salvation, to save our souls,—we remain there with our arms crossed, like that man spoken of in the Gospel. We neglect, we lose our souls. When death shall come, what shall we have to present to our Lord?

Ah! my children, hear how the good God threatens the idle: "Every tree that bringeth not forth good fruit shall be cut down, and shall be cast into the fire." "Take that unprofitable servant, and cast him out into the exterior darkness, where shall be weeping and gnashing of teeth."

Idleness is the mother of all vices. Look at the idle; they think of nothing but eating, drinking, and sleeping. They are no longer men, but stupid beasts, given up to all their passions; they drag themselves through the mire, like very swine. They are filthy, both within and without. They feed their soul only upon impure thoughts and desires. They never open their mouth but to slander their neighbour, or to speak immodest words. Their eyes, their ears, are open only to criminal objects. . . .

O my children! that we may resist idleness, let us imitate the saints. Let us watch continually over ourselves; like them, let us be very zealous in fulfilling all our duties; let the devil never find us doing nothing, lest we should yield to temptation. Let us prepare ourselves for a good death, for eternity. Let us not lose our time in lukewarmness, in negligence, in our habitual infidelities. Death is advancing; to-morrow we must, perhaps, quit our relations, our friends. Let us make haste to merit the reward promised in Paradise to the faithful servant in the Gospel!

XIII.

ON GRACE.

CAN we, of our own strength, avoid sin, and practise virtue?

No, my children, we can do nothing without the grace of God: that is an article of faith; Jesus Christ Himself taught it to us. See, the Church thinks, and all the saints have thought with her, that grace is absolutely necessary to us, and that without it we can neither believe, nor hope, nor love, nor do penance for our sins. St. Paul, whose piety was not counterfeit, assures us, on his part, that we cannot of ourselves even pronounce the Name of Jesus in a manner that can gain merit for heaven.

As the earth can produce nothing unless it is fertilised by the sun, so we can do no good without the grace of the good God.

Grace, my children, is a supernatural assistance which leads us to good ; for example, there is a sinner who goes into a church and hears an instruction: the preacher speaks of hell, of the severity of the judgments of God ; he feels himself interiorly urged to be converted ; this interior impulse is what is called grace. See, my children, it is the good God taking that sinner by the hand, and wishing to teach him to walk. We are like little children: we do not know how to walk on the road to heaven; we stagger, we fall, unless the hand of the good God is always ready to support us. O my children! how good is the good God! If we would think of all that He has done, of all that He still does every day for us, we should not be able to offend Him—we should love Him with all our heart; but we do not think of it, that is the reason. . . . . The angels sin, and are cast into hell. Man sins, and God promises him a Deliverer. What have we done to deserve this favour ? What have we done to deserve to be born in the Catholic religion, while so many souls are every day lost in other religions? What have we done to deserve to be baptised, while so many little children in France, as well as in China and America, die without baptism? What have we done to deserve the pardon of all the sins that we commit after the age of reason, while so many are deprived of the Sacrament of Penance?

O my children! St. Augustine says, and it is very true, that he seeks in us what deserves that God should abandon us, and finds it; and that he seeks what would make us worthy of His gifts, and finds nothing; because, in fact, there is nothing in us—we are nothing but ashes and sin.

All our merit, my children, consists in co-operating with grace. See, my children, a beautiful flower has no beauty nor brilliancy without the sun; for during the night it is all withered and drooping. When the sun rises in the morning, it suddenly revives and expands. It is the same with our soul, in regard to Jesus Christ, the true Sun of justice; it has no interior beauty, but through sanctifying grace. In order to receive this grace, my children, our soul must turn to the good God by a sincere conversion; we must open our hearts to Him by an act of faith and love. As the sun alone cannot make a flower expand if it is already dead, so the grace of the good God cannot bring us back to life if we will not abandon sin.

God speaks to us without ceasing by His good inspirations; He sends us good thoughts, good desires. In youth, in old age, in all the misfortunes of life, He exhorts us to receive His grace; and what use do we make of His warnings? At this moment, even, are we cooperating rightly with grace? are we not shutting the door of our heart against it? Consider that the good God will one day call you to account for what you have heard to-day; woe to you, if you stifle the cry that is rising from the depths of your conscience! We are in prosperity, we live in the midst of pleasures, all puffed up with pride; our heart is of ice towards the good God. It is a ball of copper, which the waters of grace cannot penetrate; it is a tree which receives the gentle dew, and bears no more fruit. . . .

Let us be on our guard, my children; let us take care not to be unfaithful to grace. The good God leaves us free to choose life or death; if we choose death, we shall be cast into the fire, and we must burn for ever with the devils. Let us ask pardon of God for having hitherto abused the graces He has given us, and let us humbly pray Him to grant us more.

XIV.

ON HABITUAL GRACE.

Habitual grace is a supernatural quality, divinely infused into the soul, which renders it instantly the friend of God.

This grace, my children, is given and augmented by the Sacraments, and is also kept and increased by good works; it brings the sinner to life, from being dead; it cleanses him from all the stains of sin; it bestows on his soul a beauty surpassing all that can be seen in this world; from being poor and miserable, it renders him in a moment richer than all the kings of the earth; for see, my children, the least degree of grace is worth more than all the riches of the universe, since it is a participation of the Divinity itself. From being slaves of Satan, grace makes us children of God, heirs of heaven and coheirs with Jesus Christ. In the same way that where the king is, there is his court and kingdom, so where grace is, there is the court and kingdom of God.

Yes, my children, the kingdom of God is within us when we love Him, and are in a state of grace. Our heart is the throne where the good God reposes; our thoughts, our words, our actions, directed to His glory, are His crown. We place the sceptre in the hands of the good God when we consecrate our will to Him; the love that we have for Him is His purple, His royal mantle. . . . All the joys of our soul, the members of our body, are so many vassals.

"If any man shall hear My voice and open the door to Me, I will come in to him, and will sup with him, and he with Me."

The soul, my children, is not like a servant at this feast, but like a queen, the spouse of the great King, all brilliant with beauty. . . . . A life passed thus is a foretaste of eternity.

St. Mary of Oignies, assisting once at the baptism of a little infant, perceived the Holy Ghost visibly descending into the soul of that little child, and an infinite number of angels surrounding it. What then passed visibly, my children, is done invisibly every time we receive any Sacrament. See, the angels are there, prostrate around us; they are full of admiration, they make a rampart for us of their bodies. It is said that St. Catherine of Siena went out of her house when she saw a preacher passing in the street, and went to kiss with devotion the place where he had trodden. What humility! what devotion! my children, that shows what it is to love the good God! This saint was asked one day why she did that; she answered, that our Lord had shown her the beauty of a soul which is in a state of grace, and that since then she had felt so much respect for those who consecrate themselves to the salvation of souls, that she thought it a happiness to place her lips where their feet had trod.

She used also to say, that if people could see the beauty, the ornaments of a soul in a state of grace, there would be no one who would not be ready to die a thousand times rather than lose the friendship of God by sin.

The soul enriched by grace becomes so beautiful, so pleasing to the good God, that He seems to have no eyes but to contemplate it, no ears but to hear its prayers, no mouth but to praise its beauty, no hands but to defend and support it, no arms but to caress it. . . .

What a happiness, my children, if we were already good Christians! the good God would be always with us, and we should be always with Him. . . . We could not leave Him, we should be always praying to Him in His churches, we should incessantly ask Him for His graces.

See, my children, the grace of the good God converts every thing into gold; all our actions, even the most indifferent of them, being animated by His Spirit, become works meritorious for eternal life.

A solitary one day feeling more fatigued than usual with the distance between his hut and the spring where he went to fetch water, made a resolution to bring his hut nearer to it, that he might have less trouble. As he was walking along and meditating on this project, he heard behind him a voice pronouncing these words : " One, two, three, four." It was his guardian angel counting his steps. The solitary, ashamed, instead of bringing his cell nearer, put it, on the contrary, farther off, that he might have more merit. . . .

XV.

ON PRAYER.

Our catechism teaches us, my children, that prayer is an elevation, an application of our mind and of our heart to God, to make known to Him our wants and to ask for His assistance.

We do not see the good God, my children ; but He sees us, He hears us, He wills that we should raise towards Him what is most noble in us—our mind and our heart. When we pray with attention, with humility of mind and of heart, we quit the earth, we rise to heaven, we penetrate into the Bosom of God, we go and converse with the angels and the saints.

It was by prayer that the saints reached heaven; and by prayer we too shall reach it. Yes, my children, prayer is the source of all graces, the mother of all virtues, the efficacious and universal way by which God wills that we should come to Him.

He says to us : " Ask, and you shall receive." None but God could make such promises and keep them. See, the good God does not say to us, " Ask such and such a thing, and I will grant it ;" but He says in general : " If you ask the Father any thing in My name, He will give it you."

O my children! ought not this promise to fill us with confidence, and to make us pray fervently all the days of our poor life ? Ought we not to be ashamed of our idleness, of our indifference to prayer, when our Divine Saviour, the Dispenser of all graces, has given us such touching examples of it? for you know that the Gospel tells us He prayed often, and even passed the night in prayer ? Are we as just, as holy, as this Divine Saviour ? Have we no graces to ask for ? Let us enter into ourselves ; let us consider. Do not the continual needs of our soul and of our body warn us to have recourse to Him who alone can supply them ? How many enemies to vanquish !—the devil, the world, and ourselves. How many bad habits to overcome, how many passions to subdue, how many sins to efface ! In so frightful and painful a situation, what remains to us, my children ? The armour of the saints : prayer, that necessary virtue, indispensable to good as well as to bad Christians... Within the reach of the ignorant as well as the learned, enjoined to the simple and to the enlightened, it is the virtue of all mankind; it is the science of all the faithful ! Every one on the earth who has a heart, every one who has the use of reason, ought to love and pray to God; to have recourse to Him when He is irritated; to thank Him when He confers favours; to humble themselves when He strikes.

See, my children, we are poor people, who have been taught to beg spiritually, and we do not know how to beg. We are sick people, to whom a cure has been promised, and we do not know how to ask for it. The good God does not require of us fine prayers, but prayers which come from the bottom of our heart.

St. Ignatius was once travelling with several of his companions; they each carried on their shoulders a little bag, containing what was most necessary for them on the journey. A good Christian, seeing that they were fatigued, was interiorly excited to relieve them ; he asked them as a favour to let him help them to carry their burdens. They yielded to his entreaties. When they had arrived at the inn, this man who had followed them, seeing that the Fathers knelt down at a little distance from each other to pray, knelt down also. When the Fathers rose again, they were astonished to see that this man had remained prostrate all the time they were praying; they expressed to him their surprise, and asked him what he had been doing. His answer edified them very much, for he said: "I did nothing but say, Those who pray so devoutly are saints; I am their beast of burden; O Lord! I have the intention of doing what they do; I say to Thee whatever they say." These were afterwards his ordinary words, and he arrived by means of this at a sublime degree of prayer. Thus, my children, you see that there is no one who cannot pray,—and pray at all times, and in all places; by night or by day; amid the most severe labours, or in repose; in the country, at home, in travelling. The good God is every where ready to hear your prayers, provided you address them to Him with faith and humility.

XVI.

ON THE LOVE OF GOD.[*]

"Si diligitis me, mandata mea servate."
(" If you love me, keep my commandments.")

NOTHING is so common among Christians as to say, " O my God! I love Thee," and nothing more rare, perhaps, than the love of the good God. Satisfied with making outward acts of love, in which our poor heart often has no share, we think we have fulfilled the whole of the precept. An error, an illusion ; for see, my children, St. John says that we must not love the good God in word, but in deed. Our Lord Jesus Christ also says, " If any one love Me, he will keep My Word."

If we judge by this rule, there are very few Christians who truly love God, since there are so few who keep His commandments.

Yet nothing is more essential than the love of God. It is the first of all virtues, a virtue so necessary, that without it we shall never get to heaven ; and it is in order to love God that we are on the earth. Even if the good God did not command it, this feeling is so natural to us, that our heart should be drawn to it of its own accord.

[*] Preached on Sunday, 28th May 1848.

But the misfortune is that we lavish our love upon objects unworthy of it, and refuse it to Him alone who deserves to be infinitely loved. Thus, my children, one person will love riches, another will love pleasures; and both will offer to the good God nothing but the languishing remains of a heart worn out in the service of the world. From thence comes insufficient love, divided love, which is for that very reason unworthy of the good God; for He alone being infinitely above all created good, deserves that we should love Him above all things : more than our possessions, because they are earthly ; more than our friends, because they are mortal ; more than our life, because it is perishable ; more than ourselves, because we belong to Him. Our love, my children, if it is true, must be without limit, and must influence our conduct. . . .

If the Saviour of the world, addressing Himself to each one of us separately, were now to ask us the same question that he formerly asked St. Peter : "Simon, son of John, lovest thou Me?" could we answer with as much confidence as that great Apostle, " Yea, Lord, Thou knowest that I love Thee" ?—*Domine, tu scis quia amo te.* We have perhaps pronounced these words without taking in their meaning and extent ; for, my children, to love the good

God is not merely to say with the mouth, " O my God! I love Thee !"—Oh, no ! where is the sinner who does not sometimes use this language ? . . .

To love the good God is not only to feel from time to time some emotions of tenderness towards God ; this sensible devotion is not always in our own power. To love the good God is not to be faithful in fulfilling part of our duties and to neglect the rest. The good God will have no division : " Thou shall love the Lord thy God with thy whole heart, and with thy whole soul, and with thy whole strength." This shows the strength of the commandment to love God. To love God with our whole heart is to prefer Him to every thing, so as to be ready to lose all our possessions, our honour, our life, rather than offend this good Master. To love God with our whole heart is to love nothing that is incompatible with the love of God ; it is to love nothing that can share our heart with the good God ; it is to renounce all our passions, all our ill-regulated desires. Is it thus, my children, that we love the good God ? . . .

To love the good God with our whole mind is to make the sacrifice to Him of our knowledge and our reason, and to believe all that He has taught. To love the good God with our whole mind is to think of Him often, and to make it our principal study to know Him well.

To love the good God with our whole strength, is to employ our possessions, our health, and our talents, in serving Him and glorifying Him. It is to refer all our actions to Him, as our last end. Once more, is it thus that we love the good God? Judging by this invariable rule, how few Christians truly love God! . . . .

Do those bad Christians love the good God, who are the slaves of their passions? Do those worldly persons love the good God, who seek only to gratify their body and to please the world? Is God loved by the miser, who sacrifices Him for a vile gain? Is He loved by that voluptuary, who abandons himself to vices the most opposite to divine love? Is He loved by that man who thinks of nothing but wine and good cheer? Is He loved by that other man, who cherishes an aversion to his neighbour, and will not forgive him? Is He loved by that young girl, who loves nothing but pleasures, and thinks of nothing but indulgence and vanity? No, no, my children, none of these persons love the good God; for we must love Him with a love of preference, with an active love! . . .

If we had rather offend the good God than deprive ourselves of a passing satisfaction, than

Let us go down into our own souls; let us question our hearts, my children, and see if we do not love some creature more than the good God. We are permitted to love our relations, our possessions, our health, our reputation; but this love must be subordinate to the love we should have for God, so that we may be ready to make the sacrifice of it if He should require it. . . .

Can you suppose that you are in these dispositions,—you who look upon mortal sin as a trifle, who keep it quietly on your conscience for months, for years, though you know that you are in a state most displeasing to the good God? Can you suppose that you love the good God,—you who make no efforts to correct yourselves; you who will deprive yourselves of nothing; you who offend the Creator every time that you find an opportunity? Yes, my children, what the miser loves with his whole heart is his money; what the drunkard loves with his whole heart is wine; what the libertine loves with his whole heart is the object of his passion. You, young girls, you had rather offend God than give up your finery and your vanities. You say that you love God; say rather that you love yourselves.

No, no, my children; it is not thus that the good God is to be loved, for we must love Him not only with a love of preference, but also with an active love.

"Love," says St. Augustine, "cannot remain without the constant action of the soul: *Non potest vacare amor in animâ amantis.* Yes," says this great saint; "seek for a love that does not manifest itself in works, and you will find none."

What! could it be, O my God, that Thy love alone should be barren, and that the Divine fire, which ought to enkindle the whole world, should be without activity and without strength! . . .

When you love a person, you show him more or less affection, according as the ardour of your love for him is more or less great. See, my children, what the saints were like, who were all filled with the love of the good God: nothing cost them too much; they joyfully made the greatest sacrifices; they distributed their goods to the poor, rendered services to their enemies, led a hard and penitential life; tore themselves from the pleasures of the world, from the conveniences of life, to bury themselves alive in solitude; they hastened to torments and to death, as people hasten to a feast. Such were the effects which the love of the good God produced in the saints; such ought it to produce in us. But, my children, we are not penetrated with the love of God;

we do not love the good God. Can any one say, indeed, that he loves the good God, who is so easily frightened, and who is repulsed by the least difficulty? Alas! what would have become of us if Jesus Christ had loved us only as we love Him? But no. Triumphing over the agonies of the Cross, the bitterness of death, the shame of the most ignominious tortures, nothing costs Him too dear when He has to prove that He loves us. That is our only model. If our love is active, it will manifest itself by the works which are the effects of love, because the love of the good God is not only a love of preference, but a pious affection, a love of obedience, which makes us practise His commandments; an active love, which makes us fulfil all the duties of a good Christian. Such is the love, my children, which God requires from us, to which He has so many titles, which He has purchased by so many benefits heaped upon us by His Death for us upon the Cross. What happiness, my children, to love the good God! There is no joy, no happiness, no peace, in the heart of those who do not love the good God on earth. We desire heaven, we aspire to it; but, that we may be sure to attain to it, let us begin to love the good God here below, in order to be able to love Him, to possess Him eternally, in His holy paradise. . . .

XVII.

ON PARADISE.

" Beati qui habitant in domo tuâ, Domine; in sæcula sæculorum laudabunt te."
("Blessed, O Lord, are those who dwell in Thy house.")

To dwell in the house of the good God, to enjoy the presence of the good God, to be happy with the happiness of the good God,— oh, what happiness, my children! Who can understand all the joy and consolation with which the saints are inebriated in paradise?

St. Paul, who was taken up into the third heaven, tells us that there are things above which he cannot reveal to us, and which we cannot comprehend. . . . Indeed, my children, we can never form a true idea of heaven till we shall be there. It is a hidden treasure, an abundance of secret sweetnesses, a plenitude of joy, which may be felt, but which our poor tongue cannot explain. What can we imagine greater? The good God Himself will be our recompense: *Ero merces tua magna nimis.* O God! the happiness Thou promisest us is such, that the eyes of man cannot see it, his ears cannot hear it, nor his heart conceive it.

Yes, my children, the happiness of heaven is incomprehensible; it is the last effort of the good God, who wishes to reward us. God, being admirable in all His works, will be so too when He recompenses the good Christians, who have made all their happiness consist in the possession of heaven. This possession contains all good, and excludes all evil; sin being far from heaven, all the pains and miseries which are the consequences of sin are also banished from it. No more death! . . . The good God will be in us the Principle of everlasting life. No more sickness, no more sadness, no more pains, no more grief. You who are afflicted, rejoice! your fears and your weeping will not extend beyond the grave. . . . The good God will Himself wipe away your tears! Rejoice, O you whom the world persecutes! your sorrows will soon be over, and for a moment of tribulation, you will have in heaven an immense weight of glory. Rejoice! for you possess all good things in one—the source of all good, the good God Himself.

Can any one be unhappy when he is with the good God; when he is happy with the happiness of the good God, of the good God Himself; when he sees the good God as he sees himself? As St. Paul says, my children, we shall see God face to face, because then there will be no veil between Him and us. We shall possess Him without uneasiness, for we shall no longer fear to lose Him. We shall love Him with an uninterrupted and undivided love, because He alone will occupy our whole heart.

We shall enjoy Him without weariness, because we shall discover in Him ever new perfections ; and in proportion as we penetrate into that immense abyss of wisdom, of goodness, of mercy, of justice, of grandeur, and of holiness, we shall plunge ourselves in it with fresh eagerness.

If an interior consolation, if a grace from the good God, gives us so much pleasure in this world, that it diminishes our troubles, that it helps us to bear our crosses, that it gives to so many martyrs strength to suffer the most cruel torments, — what will be the happiness of heaven, where consolations and delights are given, not drop by drop, but by torrents !

Let us represent to ourselves, my children, an everlasting day always new, a day always serene, always calm; the most delicious, the most perfect society. What joy, what happiness, if we could possess on earth, only for a few minutes, the angels, the Blessed Virgin, Jesus Christ ! In heaven we shall eternally see, not only the Blessed Virgin and Jesus Christ, we shall see the good God Himself! we shall see Him no longer through the darkness of faith, but in the light of day, in all His Majesty! . . . What happiness thus to see the good God! The angels have contemplated Him, since the beginning of the world, and they are not satiated; it would be the greatest misfortune to them to be deprived of Him for a single moment. The possession of heaven, my children, can never weary us; we possess the good God, the Author of all perfections. See, the more we possess God, the more He pleases; the more we know Him, the more attractions and charms we find in the knowledge of Him. We shall always see Him, and shall always desire to see Him; we shall always taste the pleasure there is in enjoying the good God, and we shall never be satiated with it.

The blessed will be enveloped in the Divine Immensity, they will revel in delights and be all surrounded with them, and, as it were, inebriated. Such is the happiness which the good God destines for us.

We can all, my children, acquire this happiness. The good God wills the salvation of the whole world; He has merited heaven for us by His death, and by the effusion of all His Blood. What a happiness to be able to say, "Jesus Christ died for me; He has opened Heaven for me; it is my

T

inheritance. . . . Jesus has prepared a place for me; it only depends on me to go and occupy it. *Vado vobis parare locum.* The good God has given us faith, and with this virtue we can attain to eternal life. For, though the good God wills the salvation of all men, He particularly wills that of the Christians who believe in Him: *Qui credit, habeat vitam æternam.*

Let us, then, thank the good God, my children; let us rejoice—our names are written in heaven, like those of the Apostles. Yes, they are written in the Book of Life; if we choose, they will be there for ever, since we have the means of reaching heaven.

The happiness of heaven, my children, is easy to acquire; the good God has furnished us with so many means of doing it! See, there is not a single creature which does not furnish us with the means of attaining to the good God; if any of them become an obstacle, it is only by our abuse of them. The goods and the miseries of this life, even the chastisements made use of by the good God to punish our infidelities, serve to our salvation. The good God, as St. Paul says, makes all things turn to the good of His elect; even our very faults may be useful to us; even bad examples and temptations. Job was saved in the midst of an idolatrous people. All the saints have been tempted. If these things are, in the hands of God, an assistance in reaching heaven, what will happen if we have recourse to the Sacraments, to that never-failing source of all good, to that fountain of grace supplied by the good God Himself? It was easy for the disciples of Jesus to be saved, having the Divine Saviour constantly with them. Is it more difficult for us to secure our salvation, having Him constantly with us? They were happy in obtaining whatever they wished for, whatever they chose; are we less so? We possess Jesus Christ in the Eucharist; He is continually with us, He is ready to grant us whatever we ask, He is waiting for us; we have only to ask. O my children! the poor know how to express their wants to the rich; we have only our indifference, then, to accuse, if assistance and graces are wanting to us. If an ambitious or a covetous man had as ample means of enriching himself, would he hesitate a moment, would he let so favourable an opportunity escape? Alas! we do every thing for this world, and nothing for the other! What labour, what trouble, what cares, what sorrows, in order to gather up a little fortune! See, my children, of what use are our perishable goods? Solomon, the greatest, the richest, the most fortunate of kings, said, in the height of the most brilliant fortune: " I have seen all things that are done under the sun; and behold, all is vanity and vexation of spirit."

And these are the goods to acquire which we labour so much, whilst we never think of the goods of heaven! How shameful for us not to labour to acquire it, and to neglect so many means of reaching it! If the fig-tree was cast into the fire for not having profited by the care that had been taken to render it fertile; if the unprofitable servant was reproved for having hidden the talent that he had received,—what fate awaits us, who have so often abused the aids which might have taken us to heaven? . . . If we have abused the graces that the good God has given us, let us make haste to repair the past by great fidelity, and let us endeavour to acquire merits worthy of eternal life.